ENGLISH ⌗ HERIT

Book of
Norman England

To Gwenda with much love

ENGLISH ⌗ HERITAGE

Book of
Norman
England

Trevor Rowley

B. T. Batsford / English Heritage
London

First published 1997

All rights reserved. No part of this publication
may be reproduced, in any form or by any means,
without permission from the Publisher

Typeset by Bernard Cavender Design & Greenwood Graphics Publishing
Printed and bound by The Bath Press, Bath

Published by B.T. Batsford Ltd
583 Fulham Road, London SW6 5BY

A CIP catalogue record for this book is
available from the British Library

ISBN 0 7134 8066 1 (cased)
0 7134 8060 2 (limp)

(Front cover) Goodrich Castle (English Heritage)

(Back cover) Kilpeck Church

Contents

Illustrations

Colour plates

Acknowledgements

I am most grateful to many people who have helped with the creation of this book: to Stephen Johnson for asking me to write it in the first instance and for his subsequent advice and support; to Peter Kemmis Betty and Monica Kendall at Batsford for their support and advice; to Michael Aston, Brian Durham, Diana Greenway and many others for their comments on the academic content of the book; to Richard Rowley for his help with style and for compiling the index; to Philippa Tarver, Debi Cox and Liz Miller for the production of the typescript and to those many academic visitors to Rewley House who, over the years, have enlightened me and reinforced my fascination with the Normans.

Note

County names within the text are those used pre-1974.

Introduction

On Saturday 16 October 1066:

> between the third hour and evening, the armies of Duke William of Normandy and King Harold of England met at 'the hoary appletree', and after bitter fighting and heavy casualties on both sides, 'King Harold was killed and Earl Leofwine, his brother and Earl Gyrth, his brother . . . and the French remained masters of the field'.
>
> *Anglo-Saxon Chronicle*

The Norman Conquest was the first and only successful Christian conquest of England, and brought with it a new royal dynasty, a new aristocracy, a new Church, a new art and architecture and in official circles at least, a new language.

The Norman dynasty was short lived, beginning in 1066 and finishing less than a century later in 1154. There was, however, already considerable Norman influence in England in the decades leading up to the Conquest. Emma, the daughter of Duke Richard II of Normandy, had been queen to two English kings, Aethelred (978–1016) and Cnut (1016–35), and her son, Edward the Confessor (1042–66), spent his youth in exile in Normandy (1). Both Emma and Edward were responsible for bringing a high degree of Normanization to the English court in the first half of the eleventh century.

The Norman line came to an end with the death of King Stephen, who was succeeded by the first of the Plantagenets, Henry II. However, subsequent kings adopted Norman, or rather Anglo-Norman, customs and developed Norman ideas and institutions, and many characteristics of Norman England continued well into the Middle Ages. Certainly when the English took over Ireland in the late twelfth century, that was called a 'Norman' conquest. So when did Norman England come to an end? Any date other than 1154 has to be arbitrary, but the year 1204 has much to commend it, coming as it does at the end of a century that was undoubtedly the most Norman of any century in English history. It also marked the end of the independent Duchy of Normandy, for in that year it was lost by King John to the French king, Philip Augustus.

The Norman Conquest was not a straightforward story of the imposition of a master-plan, under which the conquerors imposed their will on the conquered. There is little doubt that William I saw himself as the rightful successor to the crown and as the legitimate King of England. Most contemporary documents, including the Bayeux Tapestry, an important source of information about the Conquest, took care to emphasize this legitimacy and portray King Harold as a usurper who had broken his sacred oaths confirming William's right to the throne (**colour plate 1**).

In the first few years after becoming king, William tried to create a genuine Anglo-Norman society, where Normans and Englishmen governed alongside one another, but the various rebellions that occurred between 1068 and 1075 persuaded him that nothing less than a total Norman take-over of all the reins of power

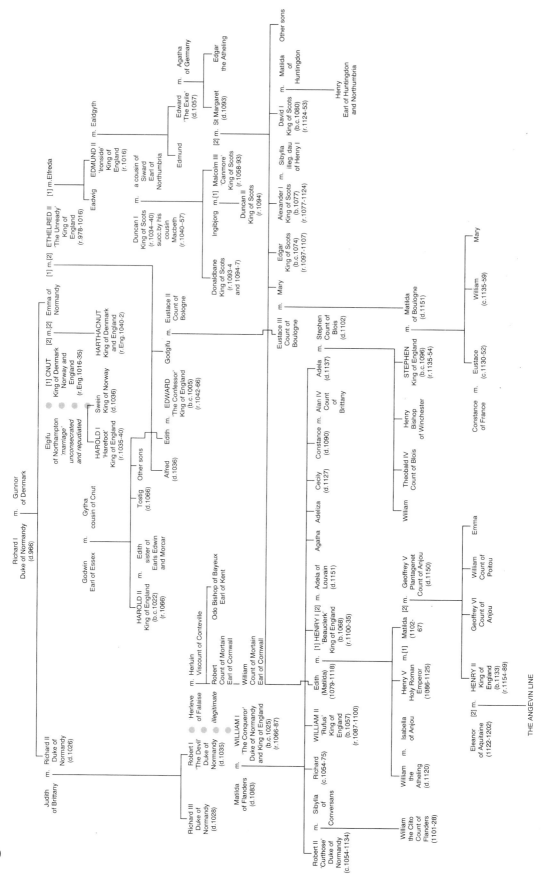

10

1 Family tree showing Norman lineage

would ensure his success as king. Consequently the second phase of Norman occupation was characterized by military suppression and plunder, during which Norman magnates and their principal tenants took over the greater part of the English landed estates. This was followed by a phase of colonization and exploitation, marked by large-scale benefactions to religious houses in Normandy. During this phase much transportable wealth and many works of art and literature were taken across the Channel into Normandy. This transfer of resources to Normandy was not entirely negative as far as England was concerned, as it helped to revive trade on both sides of the Channel; significantly the receipts of a customs post near Cherbourg increased fourteenfold between 1049 and 1093.

As the Normans settled down in the later part of the eleventh century, the movement of wealth out of the country was replaced by investment in the newly won kingdom, with new cathedrals, monasteries, churches, and military and secular buildings benefiting from Norman investment. In addition to the proliferation of castles and churches there were other more subtle consequences, such as the creation of new towns, in which migrant Normans played an important and sometimes dominant role. The Norman colonization of England was a protracted process which was essentially aristocratic, ecclesiastical and mercantile in nature, but which ended with the colonizers eventually being absorbed by the colonized, and the Normans becoming Englishmen. The contemporary historian Orderic Vitalis, who was born near Shrewsbury in 1075, and who spent most of his life as a monk in Normandy, reported that by the 1070s English and Normans were living together in boroughs, towns and cities and had intermarried. This process of intermarriage was an important factor in the eventual Anglicization of the Normans. Another historian, William of Malmesbury, writing a little later, was himself

the son of a mixed marriage and regarded such unions as commonplace, seeing them as evidence of the Normans' 'lack of prejudice'. The second generation of children of such marriages were far more likely to speak English than French, although the nobility sent their children to France in order to learn to speak French. French remained the language of the court from 1066 until the fifteenth century and after the death of Harold, English monarchs spoke in French for the next three hundred years. Henry IV (1367–1413) was the first king whose mother tongue was English. Latin, which had been used alongside Old English prior to 1066, became the written language of administration and of the Church after the Conquest. In the law courts Latin, English and Anglo-French were spoken, though court records tended to be written in Latin or French, and as a result, many legal terms which came into English from Norman French during this period remain as part of the central terminology of English law, for example 'embezzle', 'judge', 'jury', 'larceny', 'lease' and 'perjury'.

Attitudes to the Conquest

The Norman Conquest of England was an event of immense political, economic and social significance, which marked the end of Saxon England and the beginning of the Middle Ages. At least that is how the event has been portrayed by generations of historians, who have interpreted the Conquest as marking the end of the Anglo-Viking period, with its associated political confusion, and its replacement by the solidity of Norman rule. There has not, however, been any unanimity between historians about the merits of the Conquest. Sellars and Yeatman satirized one school of thought in *1066 and All That* (1930) when they humorously claimed that 'the Norman Conquest' was a 'GOOD THING', as 'from this time onward England stopped being conquered and thus was able to become top nation'. At the other end of the spectrum there have been those historians who have emphasized the negative aspects of Norman culture. Pre-eminent in this group was Sir Frank Stenton, who, in his magisterial *Anglo-Saxon England* (1943), wrote: 'in comparison with England, Normandy in the mid eleventh century was still a state in the making', and that the Normans were 'a harsh and violent race, they were the closest of all western people to the Barbarian strain in the continental order. They had produced little in art or learning and nothing in literature that could be set beside the work of Englishmen.'

The concept of the 'Norman Yoke' has been articulated in a wide range of historical and political writings from the seventeenth century onwards. Sir Henry Spelman (died 1641) and Sir Robert Cotton (died 1631) traced many legal abuses back to the Normans and the feudal system, a theme taken up and developed by nineteenth-century romantic writers such as Charles Kingsley and George Borrow. Their central thesis was that before 1066 the Saxons had lived as free and equal citizens, governed by means of representative institutions. The Norman Conquest was responsible for depriving the English of these liberties, establishing the tyranny of an alien king and landlords. Theories of this nature were almost certainly current throughout the Middle Ages and account for the popularity of Edward the Confessor, both as king and as saint, and of King Alfred, who came to assume the role of a symbol of national independence. The simplicity of this interpretation undoubtedly accounts for its longevity, but as a historical analysis of the Conquest and subsequent history it leaves much to be desired. Saxon England was already divided into hierarchical social groupings, and although it remained popular to attribute all the problems that England experienced after 1066 to 'the French Bastard and his banditti' (Thomas Paine), it is as inadequate an explanation of events in the eleventh and twelfth centuries as that presented by Sellars and Yeatman. Many scholars are now anxious to emphasize the essential continuum of life before and after 1066.

This was the view held by perhaps the greatest of all the historians of Norman England, E. A. Freeman, who in his monumental *History of the Norman Conquest of England: Its Causes and its Results* (1867–79), identified a basic continuity in English society: 'The fiery trial which England went through was a fire which did not destroy, but only purified. She came forth once more the England of old.'

The archaeological perspective

Archaeologists, reliant on the surviving physical evidence, have tended to be more conservative in their attitude to the Conquest. While recognizing the fundamental importance of the introduction and spread of castle fortifications and of Romanesque architecture under the Normans, they have been much more circumspect about the Norman impact on Saxon England. In particular they have pointed out the continuity in the surviving physical record, ranging from pottery to coinage, where the influence of the new Norman dynasty was almost imperceptible. William, like an earlier conqueror, Cnut, adjusted the weight of silver in their pennies, probably in order to extract higher tax returns, but otherwise maintained Saxon coinage conventions (**2**). Both William and his successors took care to keep the English and Norman currencies separate. The English coinage was melted down and reminted in Normandy, and hence few Saxon or Anglo-Norman coins have been found in the Duchy, and vice versa.

Some archaeologists have claimed that without the documentary sources which catalogue the Conquest and its aftermath, it would be difficult to detect the coming of the Normans at all. The graphic military events so vividly portrayed on the Bayeux Tapestry find few echoes in the below-ground evidence, and the massive transfer of land and power so painstakingly recorded in the folios of Domesday Book (1086) (**3**) is rarely reflected in the stratigraphy and artefacts of the second half of the eleventh century. The Conquest marked

2 Part of a rare find of a hoard of nine silver pennies of William the Conqueror, from Norwich. The Normans used the same design for their coinage as that used of the late Saxon kings; this was one method by which they emphasized the continuity of the royal lineage. (British Museum)

an exchange of aristocracy, rather than a folk movement, and as only a relatively small number of Norman barons were involved it is only at the upper end of the social spectrum that archaeologists would expect to find much evidence of Normanization. Indeed the Normans were not responsible for introducing new technological innovations; agricultural and industrial practices remained much the same after 1066 as they were before, and for the most part artefacts continued to evolve in style – there was no revolution. One might have expected the turmoil brought by the Conquest to have resulted in the deposition of coin hoards as in previous and later periods of political disruption, but with the exception of a hoard of nine silver pennies of William the Conqueror deposited *c*. 1069 in Norwich, so far such evidence has yet to be recovered.

It can perhaps be argued that archaeology is a weak medium to catalogue subtle changes in power and society over such a relatively short period. However, in recent years archaeological investigation, both above and below ground, has begun to produce evidence of important developments in the eleventh and particularly the twelfth century. For instance, it has been shown that increasingly specialized butchery techniques, identified in the bone evidence from Lincoln, were the result of the influx of French colonists and soldiers in the late eleventh century. The broader landscape evidence also points consistently towards a centralization of political and commercial power which led to a campaign of building and rebuilding that could only be associated with a radical change in society. It also led to the establishment of many new towns and villages and the redesign of others, reflecting increased prosperity and seigneurial control which to a large extent must be attributed to the coming of the Normans.

The making of Normandy

In order to understand the Normans more fully, it is necessary to look at their origins. During the eighth century the Frankish empire emerged to occupy most of what is now France, a large part of Germany, Austria and the Low Countries. It reached its height under the Emperor Charlemagne, who was crowned the

OXENEFSCIRE.

·I· TERRA ARCHIEPI CANTVARIENS'.

ARCHIEPS CANTVAR' ten' NEWTONE. De pecefsun
7 e'. Ibi fe. xx. hide. Tpa. e. xcvii. car'.
Ne in dnio. vi. car' 7 v. seruo 7 xxii. uilti cu. x. bord' hnt
xii. car'. Ibi. xv. ac' pra. 7 ii. querne pasture. Silua
una leu' lg. 7 una lat'. Cu onerat' ual. xx v. solid.
De hac tra ten' Rotb' de odgi. i. hid. 7 Rogeri'. i. hid.
T.R.E. ualb. xii. lib. modo. xv. lib.

·II· TERRA EPI WINTONIENSIS.

EPS WINTON ten' SVTENIE. Grag and tenuit
Ibi fe. xxx. hide. Tpa. e. xx. iii. car'. Ne in dnio
x. car' 7 xx. seruo. 7 xxx vi. uilti cu. xi. bord' hnt xx.
car'. Ibi. ii. molin' de xxxii. sol' 7 vi. den'. 7 c. ac' pra.
Silua. iii. leu' lg. 7 ii. leu' lat'. Cu onerat' ual. l. sol.
T.R.E. ualb. xii. lib. modo. xxv. lib.

Ide' eps ten' EBVRGEBERIE. De eccla fun' 7 e.
Ibi fe. xcii. hide 7 dim. Tpa. e. xx. car'.
Ne in dnio. iii. car' 7 xx. seruo. 7 xx vii. uilti cu. xx. bord'
hnt. xxx. car'. Ibi. ii. molin' de. xx. sol'. 7 xx vi. ac'
pra. de x. sol. Tot. iii. leu' 7 iii. qc lg. 7 i. leu' 7 dim lat'.
T.R.E. ualb. xii. lib. modo. xx. lib.

·III· TERRA EPI SARISBERIENS'.

EPS SARISBER' ten' DVNESMENE. De eccla fuit 7 e.
Ibi fe. xxx. hide. Tpa. e. xx. car'. Ne in dnio. ii. car'.
7 xl. uilti cu. xcvi. bord' hnt xx. car'. 7 ibi. i. seruus.
7 l. ac' pra. Silua. i. leu' 7 iiii. qc lg. 7 dim leu' lat'.
Valuer 7 ual. xx. lib.

·V· TERRA EPI DE EXECESTRE.

EPS EXONIENS' ten' de rege. vi. hid in BENTONE.
7 Rotbgo' de eo. Leuric eps tenuit. Tpa. e. vi. car'.
Ne in dnio. ii. car' 7 ii. seruo. 7 x. uilti cu. vi. bord' hnt
iii. car'. Ibi. ii. piscarie de. xxxiii. sol. 7 xl vii. ac' pra.
T.R.E. ualb. iiii. lib. modo. vi. lib.

·VI· TERRA EPI LINCOLIENSIS. In Dorchecestre IX

EPS LINCOLIENS' ten' DORCHECESTRE. Ibi sun'
.c. hide. x. min'. De his tra eps in sua firma. lxb hd'
una v min'. 7 milites xxx. hid 7 una v'.
Ne in dnio tra. iiii. car'. Sed. iii. car' tanm fo. xxx vii.
uilti cu. xxii. bord' hnt. xv. car'. Ibi molin' de. xx. sol.
piscator redd. xxx. sticl' anguill. 7 usi tra. xii. sol. p dm'
hida. De pra. xl. solid. Silua minuta. vi. qc' 7 ii. lat'
Iper lege redd hoc m. xxx. lib p ann. T.R.E. ualb. xviii. lib.
De ead tra huj m ten' Bristeua. xx. hid 7 dim ad
firma. Tpa. e. xxvi. car'. Ne in dnio. iii. car' 7 xl vi. uilti
cu. xv. bord' hnt. xx. car'. Ibi. iiii. molin' de. xxxviii. sol.
De pra' piscarius. xcvi. sol. 7 vii. den'. 7 x. sticl' anguill.
p qr tra redd ista tra. xx. lib. T.R.E. x. lib. Cu recep. viii. lib.
In hac ead tra epi in Sioch .xvii. hd 7 una v ge.

De his hid. viii. so in dnio. 7 ibi. ii. car'. 7 xii. uilti cu. v. bord'
7 i. seruo hnt. vii. car'. Ibi. xxiii. ac' pra.
Valuit. vi. lib. T.R.E. in redd. xii. lib. 7. xii. sticl' anguill.

Ipse eps ten' TAME. Ibi fe. lx. hide. De his tra in firma
tua. xxx vii. hid. 7 milites eb hnt alias. Tpa. e. xxiii.
car'. Ne in dnio. v. car' 7 v. seruo. 7 xx vii. uilti cu. xx vi. bord'
hnt. xix. car'. Ibi molin' de. xx. sol. De pra'. lx. solid.
T.R.E. ualb. xx. lib. Cu recep. xvii. lib. Modo. xxx. lib.

Ide' eps ten' CLIDELICOME. Ibi fe. xl. hide. De his tra in sua
firma. xxx i. hd'. 7 milites alias. Tpa. e. xxvi. car'.
Ne in dnio. v. car'. 7 xx iii. uilti cu. xxx i. bord' 7 ptro hnt
xix. car'. Ibi molin' de. xv. sol. 7 pru de. x. sol.
T.R.E. 7 post ualb. xviii. lib. modo. xxx. lib.

Ipse eps ten' BANESBERIE. Ibi fe. l. hide. De his tra eps
in dnio tra. x. car'. 7 iii. hid. 7 dol' uilte. xxx iii. hid 7 dim'.
T.R.E. epuit ibi. xxx iii. car' 7 dim' 7 ead eps'. B. muent.
Ne in dnio. vii. car'. 7 xxiii. seruo. 7 lxx vi. uilti cu. xvii. bord'
hnt. xxx iii. car'. Ibi. iii. molin' de. xl v. solid. pastura tra
iii. quern' lg. 7 ii. qc lat'.
T.R.E. ualet. xxx v. lib. Cu recep. xxx. lib. Modo ual' idem.

Ipse eps ten' CROPELIE. De eccla a Lucol fuit 7 e.
Ibi fe. l. hide. De his tra eps in firma. xxx v. hd. 7 milites tnut
Sup has. l. hd. e' tra in dnio ad. x. car'. Inr eos tra. e. xxx. car'.
Eps muent. xxx v. Ne in dnio. vi. car'. 7 xii. seruo. 7 l v.
uilti cu. xcii. bord' hnt. xxx iii. car'. Ibi. ii. molin' de. xxviii. sol.
7 c. xx. ac' pra. 7 c. xxxii. ac' pastura.
T.R.E. ualb. xx viii. lib. Cu recep' xxx. lib. Modo ual' idem.

Ipse eps ten' EALESHAM. 7 Coluban' monach' de eo. Ibi fe.
xv. hide. 7 dim' pan' eb ecole.
Tpa. e. xxix. car' 7 uat' muent. In dnio. e tra. vi. car' inland
Ne in dnio. iii. car'. 7 iii. milites cu. xxx iii. uillis 7 xxxii. bord'
hnt. xxii. car'. Ibi molin' de. xii. sol. 7 cccc l. anguill. 7 c. l v.
ac' pra. 7 c. ac' pastura. Silua. i. leu' 7 iii. qc lg. 7 i. leu' 7 ii. qc lat'.
Cu onerat' ual. xx v. sol. Valuer 7 ual. xx. lib.
De Coluban' ten' de eps Suptone. Ibi fe. iii. hide. Tpa. e. v.
car'. Ne in dnio. i. car' 7 vii. uilti cu. v. bord' hnt. v. car'.
Ibi. l. ac' pra. 7 pastur' i qc lg. 7 i. qc lat'.
7 cc l. anguill 7 in sol 7 iiii. den'. Valuer. iii. lib. modo c. solid.
De Coluban' ten' de eps v. hd' in parua TOLLENDONE.
7 pan' ad ecclam. Tpa. e. vi. car'. In dnio fe. ii. car'. 7 ii. seruo.
7 xii. uilti cu. iii. bord' hnt. vi. car'. Ibi. xx v. ac' pra Valuer
7 ual c. sol.

De tra DORCHECESTRE ten' angli. Ibi hoct. iii. hd' 7 dim'
7 Conan. viii. hd' una v min'. Walcher. vi. hd' 7 dim' 7 seuuad'
v. hid' 7 dim'. Iacob. i. hd'. Rainald' 7 vitat'. v. hd'
Tpa e' xx. car'. Ibi fe' in dnio. xx. car' 7 xx vi. uilti cu. v. bord'
7 iii. seruo hnt. xx vi. car'. 7 ibi hnt uni so. l. ac' pra.
Tot T.R.E. ualb. xx v. lib. Cu recep' xxii. lib. modo. xxx v. lib.

3 An extract from the folios of Domesday Book (1086) showing the Oxfordshire land held from King William by the Archbishop of Canterbury and the Bishops of Winchester, Salisbury, Exeter and Lincoln. (Public Records Office)

first Holy Roman Emperor in Rome in 800. The Carolingian empire was politically and militarily powerful, and was associated with a European cultural renaissance in art and scholarship. Nevertheless, on Charlemagne's death in 814, the empire which he had extended into Spain, Italy and Saxony began the long process of disintegration, under attack from within and from the Vikings in the North and from the Moslems in the South. Eventually in the middle of the ninth century, the crumbling empire was divided into east and west, essentially covering Germany and France respectively.

Viking attacks on western Europe continued, and in England resulted in the establishment of Scandinavian political and cultural dominance in a region known as the Danelaw, while in continental Europe the Vikings using the great western river estuaries were able to penetrate the disintegrating empire. Although the Vikings established short-lived areas of political control around the mouths of the Rivers Rhine and Loire, it was only in Normandy that they were able to create a Scandinavian political territory similar to that embedded in England. The estuary of the River Seine provided ready access to central France, and in the ninth century the Vikings raided as far east as Paris and beyond. Norsemen overran the Seine valley, looting and burning churches, monasteries and villages in the process. Eventually the western emperor, Charles the Simple, was obliged to concede a large area around the Seine estuary to a Viking called Rollo, and Normandy was born at a treaty signed at St Clair-sur-Epte (911). Rollo converted to Christianity and acted as guard for the Franks against other marauders in the Seine valley. The abdication of royal authority enabled him to establish a line of hereditary counts who were later known as dukes. Paris was spared further

attacks, and Normandy developed to become the greatest of the Frankish principalities (**4**). In 924 and 933 further territory was passed to the Normans, and by the middle of the tenth century the Terra Northmannoran or Northmannia had been fully established.

Despite its origins as a Frankish marcher territory under Scandinavian mercenary control, the Duchy of Normandy rapidly assumed the characteristics of contemporary French principalities. Many Carolingian governmental institutions survived, and despite the influx of large numbers of Scandinavian settlers in the first half of the tenth century, the Duchy of Normandy rapidly assumed a French character. Intermarriage, several decades of social stability and considerable Frankish migration to Normandy helped to assimilate the Scandinavian settlers, and by the time of the conquest of England the Scandinavian language had virtually ceased to be spoken in the Duchy. The Duchy of Normandy was a mixture of Roman, Carolingian, Frankish and Scandinavian elements, with contributions from others such as the Italians. This blend of cultures created an immensely powerful political and military player on the eleventh-century European stage.

Normandy and the Conquest

The new Scandinavian rulers of Normandy readily adopted Christianity, but there is little evidence of any major Church renaissance in the Duchy during the tenth century, in the form of cathedral, church or abbey construction. Ironically the Normans did refound a number of abbeys, such as St Wandrille, Rouen and Jumièges (**5**), which their ancestors had been responsible for destroying. However, when in 996 Richard II became duke, an era of relative peace and prosperity began. Richard was noted for his patronage of the Church and invited William of Volpiano (died 1031) from Burgundy to the Norman coastal power-base at Fécamp to help transform the Norman Church. William was an energetic monk from Cluny,

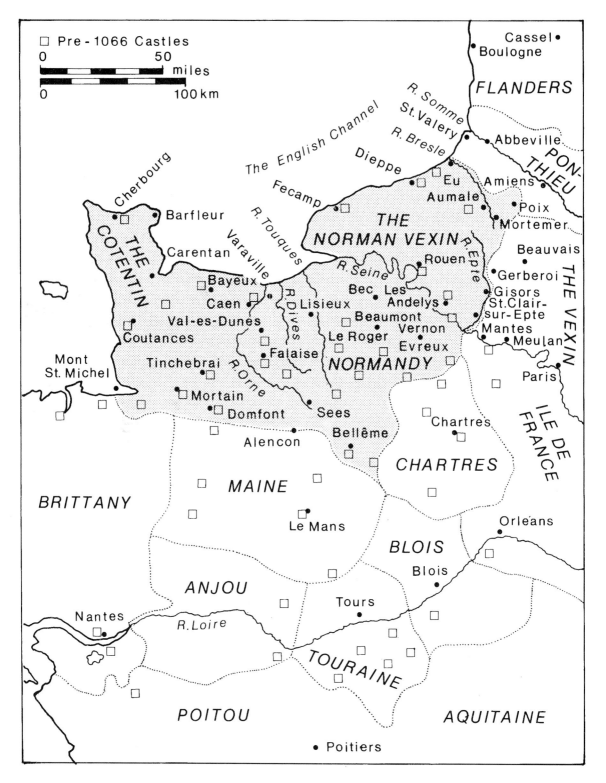

□ Pre - 1066 Castles

0   50
▮▮▮▮▮▮▮▮ miles
0   100 km

Cassel •
Boulogne •

FLANDERS

R. Somme
St. Valery

PON-
THIEU

Abbeville •

The English Channel

Dieppe

R. Bresle

Amiens

Fecamp

Eu

Aumale

Poix

Cherbourg

Barfleur •

R. Touques

THE
NORMAN VEXIN

Mortemer

THE
COTENTIN

Carentan

Varaville

R. Seine

Rouen

Beauvais

Gerberoi

R. Epte

THE VEXIN

Bec Les

Gisors

St.Clair-
sur-Epte

Bayeux

R. Dives

Lisieux

Andelys

Caen

Beaumont

Mantes

Val-es-Dunes

Le Roger

Vernon

Meulan

Coutances

Falaise

NORMANDY

Evreux

Paris

Mont
St. Michel

Tinchebrai

R. Orne

Mortain

Domfont

Sees

Chartres

ILE DE FRANCE

Alencon

Belleme

BRITTANY

MAINE

CHARTRES

Le Mans

Orleans

BLOIS

ANJOU

Blois

Nantes

R. Loire

Tours

TOURAINE

POITOU

AQUITAINE

• Poitiers

4 Map of north-western France in the eleventh century showing the location of the Duchy of Normandy and its neighbours. (Judith Dobie)

which at that time was the focal point of western Christianity, and once established in the Duchy he used Fécamp as a centre to revitalize the Norman Church. He reorganized the diocesan infrastructure and founded a number of new monastic institutions – there was an increase from just five in 1000 to over thirty in 1066. William's work had a fundamental impact on the role that the Church played in Norman society, and during the first half of the eleventh century the reformed Norman Church was to gain a European-wide reputation for scholarship, capable of attracting other influential recruits from outside the Duchy. The most significant of these was another Italian, Lanfranc (died 1089), who transformed the abbey at Le Bec-Héllouin from relative obscurity to one of the most famous monasteries in Europe. Pupils from many countries were attracted there by its reputation for learning (6). Two of the most notable were Anselm of Lucca,

5 The monumental ruins of the church of Notre-Dame, which formed the centrepiece of the abbey at Jumièges on the River Seine in Normandy. The construction of the abbey church was started in 1051 by Abbot Robert, who later became Archbishop of Canterbury. Jumièges and Edward the Confessor's church at Westminster Abbey had many similar design features.

who was later to become Pope Alexander II and thus further tie the Norman cause closely to the papacy, and Anselm of Aosta, a formidable intellectual who was also to become Archbishop of Canterbury in 1093.

The new foundations became centres of prestige, wealth, learning and spiritual excellence, and established a direct link with the great monasteries of Burgundy, northern Italy and Rome. Lanfranc acted as Duke William's ecclesiastical agent in developing and strengthening the episcopacy and forging it as a major tool of government. By appointing

6 A portrait of Lanfranc, Archbishop of Canterbury (1070–89) from a contemporary document in the Bodleian Library, Oxford.

William's nominees, such as his half-brother Odo as Bishop of Bayeux in 1049, Lanfranc was able to guarantee the allegiance of the Church to the duke and most importantly to his military campaigns. Along with the newly reformed Church came a new architectural style, derived from Italy, Burgundy and Germany, and by the 1050s new abbey churches were under construction at Mont-St-Michel, Rouen, Jumièges and Caen, all adopting the style called simply Roman in France and Norman or Romanesque in England.

The Normans' pre-eminence at Hastings paradoxically derived largely from the fact that from about 1025 Normandy itself had been disturbed by warfare within its ruling classes. This unrest was a result of a feudal revolution and was accompanied as in other regions in France with castle building and the subjugation of previously free landholders. During this phase some families left the Duchy, but more importantly others moved in. It is worth noting that few of the great Norman families that featured prominently in later English affairs had acquired their Norman lands before 1030. In the army that won at Hastings were knights from Brittany, Flanders, Artois and Picardy. Thus the Normans formed the vanguard of a wider movement of Frankish conquest. Many of these 'foreign' soldiers had been assimilated into the Norman aristocracy only in the three decades before the Conquest. Just as Normandy created a new Church in the eleventh century, so it created a new nobility, with new migrant families such as the Beaumonts, Bohuns and Warrennes assuming a central role. The Franks brought military methods to Normandy based on cavalry and castles which when tied to social changes created a feudal dominance that was to prove particularly potent in England.

ELLVM: AT·HESTENGA CEASTRA

The Norman conquest of England was in some ways a repeat of the Scandinavian conquest of Normandy. The Scandinavians in Normandy proved themselves to be adaptable, using the institutions they found and developing them to create a well-ordered state. They recognized the need to import both men and ideas from outside the Duchy and in this context were responsible for attracting large numbers of soldiers, scholars and clerics from throughout Europe. In particular, their ability to attract clerics of the calibre of Anselm and Lanfranc transformed the Norman Church into a powerful and respectable

7 William the Conqueror shown holding the papal banner while directing the building of Hastings Castle before the battle of Hastings on the Bayeux Tapestry. The support of Pope Alexander II reinforced the Norman claim that the conquest of England was a holy war.

institution. The newly formed Church was able to create an environment in which the conquest of England was perceived as a holy war, blessed by the papacy. Throughout the battle of Hastings on the Bayeux Tapestry, Duke William is portrayed holding the papal banner as confirmation that this was a just and holy war (7).

1
Saxon England in the eleventh century

The England William conquered was an old and well-established country with its own distinctive institutions and cultures. Domesday Book (1086) provides us with a snapshot of late Saxon England. It portrays a country well settled and cultivated with thousands of rural settlements and over one hundred towns. It points to a sophisticated local government system, superior perhaps to anything to be found in contemporary Europe and capable of providing the Normans with the administrative infrastructure to rule the country.

For many people 1066 did not mark a dramatic break with what had gone before, and their way of life remained largely unaltered after the Conquest. Their work, their houses, their food, their utensils, their games and even the way they dressed would not have been noticeably different, at least not to begin with. Nevertheless England before the Conquest was a culturally divided country, with a largely Saxon population occupying the southern and central regions, and a largely Anglo-Scandinavian population occupying the North and East. In the West and North there was a strong Celtic culture, not only in Wales and Scotland, but also along the borders of England and in the South-West. Even within these broad cultural areas there were distinct regional characteristics. By the eighth century the numerous Anglo-Saxon kingdoms that had emerged in the post-Roman period had dwindled to three dominant Christian principalities: Northumbria in the North, Mercia in the Midlands and Wessex in the South. These three fought for the dominance of England until the coming of the Vikings in the eighth century. The pagan Vikings conquered Northumbria and much of Mercia, invasion was followed by settlement, and there was a fusion of Anglo-Saxon and Scandinavian societies.

The North (and indeed many other parts of England) was subjected to repeated Viking attacks in the eighth, ninth and tenth centuries, but as the Saxon kingdom of Wessex in the South grew in strength and began to regain territory lost to the Scandinavians, the nature of the incursions changed from invasion followed by settlement to military activity of a largely political nature. This was led by the Danes intent on wresting power from the newly dominant Saxon kings of Wessex. The Anglo-Scandinavian society that developed in the North had elements of both groups within it. Scandinavian language, place-names and institutions figured largely, but as the community began to return to Christianity governmental structures were established which owed something to both cultures.

Under Alfred the Great, King of the West Saxons (871–99), and his successors the Danelaw was reconquered and eventually divided into shires on the Wessex pattern, and thus by the end of the tenth century there was a loosely knit but durable English kingdom with a unified taxation and coinage system. Royal control developed steadily with a sophisticated administration that established a judicial system based on the royal court imposing its writ throughout the counties, using a network of local officers and courts which in turn led to a decline in the importance of regional tribal laws, which had been dominant previously. Significantly the affairs of the courts were transacted in the English language throughout the country despite the fact that there were three Danish kings of England in the eleventh century.

Saxon administration

By 1066, with the exception of Rutland, Lancashire and the north-western counties, the shire system of England had been established. Some of the counties were very ancient: those of the kingdom of Wessex – Hampshire, Wiltshire, Dorset, Devon, Somerset – were in existence at least by the late eighth century. Some, such as Essex, Kent and Sussex, were former kingdoms, while the Midland shires were established for taxation purposes in the tenth century. This national system of counties was to form the basis of English local government for a millennium (8).

The shires were sub-divided into units known as hundreds, which in theory consisted of a hundred hides; the hide was a smaller unit of agrarian organization. In the Danelaw the equivalents of the hundreds were known as wapentakes. All free tenants were entitled to attend the Hundred Court, which met monthly, and was initially intended to transact local business. From the tenth century the court was used increasingly as a means of extending royal government to the countryside, and the hundreds appear to have assumed military responsibilities. In some documents the term 'hundred' is synonymous with *fyrd*. The Saxon *fyrd* was a military force made up of all free men who, unless exempted by special privilege, were required to help in the upkeep of the fortified towns known as *burhs* and provide other general defensive duties. There has been much debate about how far the military

obligations of those who served in the *fyrd* resembled the feudal obligations later imposed on the inhabitants of Norman England. The Danish kings had households consisting of retainers called housecarls, and some of these men were also given estates in return for military service. Thus by the tenth century military obligations and service were being developed to provide a system of royal defence, which included a new weapon, the fleet, and it is clear from many sources that significant elements of feudalism were present in pre-Conquest England.

During the tenth century the basic social structure of the English village had also been established, with different systems operating in the Danelaw and the Saxon-dominated areas. The manorial system, which was at the core of Norman feudalism, did not exist before the Conquest, but the Saxon social structure was also a hierarchical one consisting of slaves, ceorls (free peasants with their own land), gesiths, thegns (lords owning a church, a gatehouse and five hides of land according to the laws of King Cnut) and the great lords of each shire, the ealdormen. By the eleventh century ealdormen had been replaced by their Scandinavian equivalent, the earls, whose authority extended over several shires and who were like local kings under the king himself. The English thegns wielded considerable power and influence and contributed most of the tax in late Saxon England; they were the equivalent of the post-Conquest manorial lords, although their responsibilities and duties were not as clearly defined as those of their successors. In the Danelaw there was a complex social structure of lords, tenants and free peasants. The early Saxon system of justice by blood feud had been gradually replaced by that of 'wergeld', that is a fine or compensation. The structure of county, hundred and local courts, with the Danelaw tradition of juries of twelve men, was taken over by the Normans, as was the office of 'shire-reeve', or sheriff, the king's representative in each county.

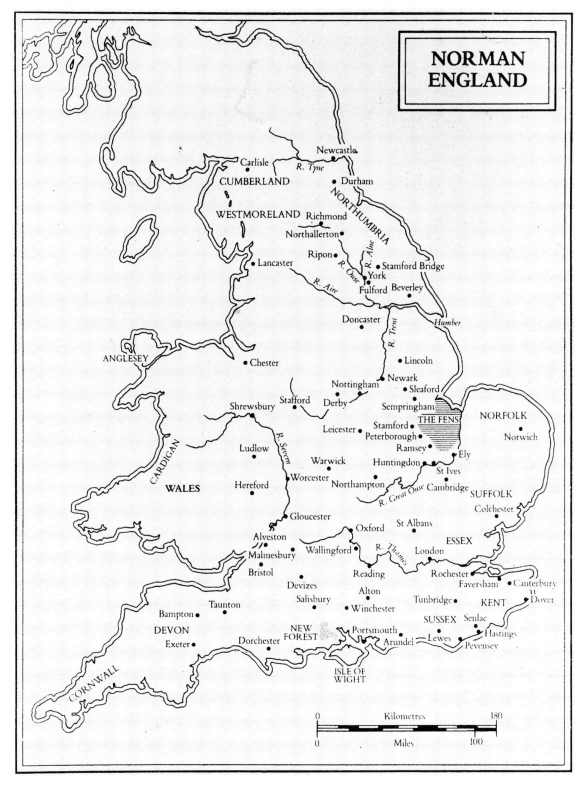

8 Map of Norman England. (After Loyn)

9 Aerial view of Wallingford (Berks.), showing the line of defences of the Saxon *burh*, together with the outline of the Saxon street plan. William and his army crossed the Thames (bottom right) here in 1066 and built a castle in the north-eastern segment of the Saxon town (top right).

The towns of Saxon England

Despite the political turbulence and general unrest in the tenth and early eleventh centuries, the late Saxon period saw the continued development of urban communities in England. Town life in England had all but disappeared in the post-Roman period, but gradually re-emerged in the form of trading centres or *wics* in the mid-Saxon era. These nascent towns were largely destroyed by Viking activity or the threat of it, and in response to this King Alfred and his successors established a network of fortified settlements in southern England. Some of these *burhs* (such as Winchester (Hants) were based on Roman towns, while others, such as Wallingford (Berks.) (9) and Wareham (Dorset), occupied new sites, normally located in order to protect an important river crossing. The defences of the newly established *burhs* tended to be built of earth and timber, and can still be traced in earthwork form in several towns, while at towns such as Winchester, Chichester and Bath, the old Roman walls were reinforced. At Winchester and many other *burhs* the basic street plan also dates from the Alfredian era and, for example, analysis of Oxford's medieval street plan shows that it was created at the same time as its burghal defences (10). The concept of the fortified town was replicated in Mercia, where indeed it may have originated, and later on by the Anglo-Vikings in the Danelaw. The *burhs* provided security for trade and commerce that encouraged the development of a considerable number of thriving towns in late Anglo-Scandinavian England. In all there were 112 places which were defined as boroughs by the late eleventh century.

Even the largest towns, including London, were firmly wedded to the countryside they serviced. All Anglo-Saxon towns included some arable land, and most contained within their walls a substantial proportion of agricultural workers, who were often described in the Domesday survey as if they were regular manorial peasantry. Cambridge, for instance, was a significant settlement with a total population of at least 1600 in 1086. Nevertheless, the agrarian basis of the community was emphasized by the burgesses lending the sheriff their plough teams three times a year. In the eleventh century there was therefore often little distinction between town and country or indeed between small town and village. There were a multitude of small boroughs that were more agricultural than urban in nature and a host of villages with markets that nevertheless could not be classified as boroughs. Occasionally, Domesday provides us with direct evidence of the initial break itself

being made. For instance, Tutbury (Staffs.) was the head of the powerful honour of Henry of Ferrers, where Domesday records that in the *burh* around the castle there were forty-two men living by their trade alone.

There are no surviving examples of above-ground Saxon town houses, although excavations have revealed their outline plans in several places such as London, Northampton, Lincoln and Durham. These buildings were mainly of timber, but they infrequently survive even in archaeological form, and the local urban topography has to be deduced from the distribution of the rubbish pits and cesspits which served them. At Watling Court in London, properties appear to have been physically separate units from as early as the late ninth century as defined by the evidence of

10 The plan of Oxford's Saxon defences and street plan. The original *burh* was extended to the east in the late Saxon period. (Judith Dobie)

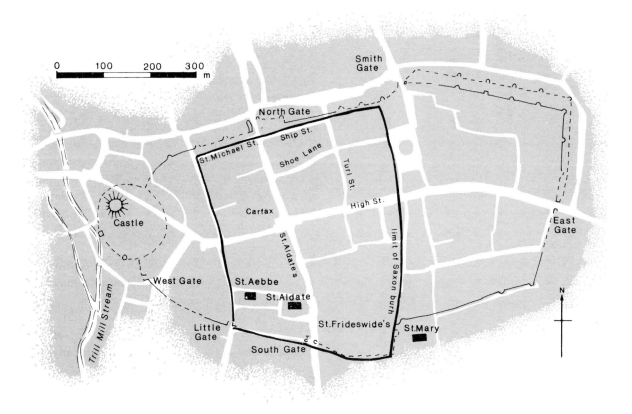

pits spaced at regular intervals. Excavated properties along Bow Lane, *c*. 1050, have also been interpreted as a street-range of regularly constructed timber buildings, and their density implies a high population concentration. These excavations also demonstrate the emergence of the common right-angled medieval town-house plan by the mid-eleventh century. Such buildings normally incorporated a sunken cellar. At Northampton on St Peter's Street there was evidence of a reorganization of streets and buildings into a regular rectilinear arrangement replacing a looser earlier configuration. At Durham fenced boundaries were established towards the rear of Saxon properties, presumably parcelling out a back-land which had previously been common and was the site of large rubbish pits. Such excavations all point to a high degree of urban organization in the late Saxon period. At London and Winchester stone buildings have been identified from as early as *c*. 1100, but evidence of specialist buildings such as alehouses and shops is rare in late Saxon England.

Pottery is an essential tool for the medieval archaeologist, yet pottery production in late Saxon England was very unevenly spread. In the western part of the kingdom there were large areas where little or no pottery was produced or used, while in the North-East, Midlands and eastern England there was widespread use of high-quality wheel-thrown pottery. The Stamford and Thetford varieties were the most common and showed the greatest degree of industrialization. At least some of these centres were producing pottery in England in the ninth century, but most were encouraged as a result of the trading activities of the new late Saxon towns.

Similar pottery came somewhat later in the south of England, but by the eleventh century its manufacture was well established in a number of centres. The fact that most of these industries were located in towns probably reflects the expansion of urban markets over much of England, from the late ninth century, as well as the attempts by the later Saxon kings to limit trading to towns by legislation. All these industries employed techniques of a higher degree of sophistication than had hitherto been used in these regions, and all produced a range of vessel forms already widely made in northern Europe. It seems likely that both the form and the manufacturing techniques were introduced by immigrant potters attracted both by the large populations in the East and North-East and by the growth of towns over all England in the tenth century. The general differences in form between the rounded or baggy types in the South and the taller shapes made in the East and North-East also suggest that these potters came from two different areas – from the Rhineland to East Anglia, Lincolnshire and Yorkshire in the ninth and early tenth centuries, and probably from northern France to the south of England in the later tenth and eleventh centuries. The Conquest did not result in any change to pottery types in the short term, although there was a steady increase in the amount of imported wares from the Continent from the twelfth century (**11**). There were also longer-term changes in the structure of the pottery industry. The lack of any significant change in pottery styles in the eleventh century does pose a problem for the archaeologist trying to detect evidence of Norman activity in many contexts, but particularly in rural settlements.

Anglo-Norman coinage

At the heart of late Saxon town life were the shire capitals, which were royal boroughs. Two-thirds of the proceeds of justice and dues and customs went to the king and one-third to the earl. Such boroughs possessed a mint, which brought in substantial revenue to the crown. The late Saxon system of coinage, which was the most sophisticated in Europe, had been introduced by King Edgar (957/9–75). There was only one denomination, the silver penny; smaller change was provided by cutting pennies into halves and quarters. Coinage had a uniform appearance as the same coin was issued

simultaneously at all mints and standards were closely regulated. Each coin was inscribed with the name of the mint and the moneyer responsible for issuing it. Coinage was in itself a means of taxation as coin types were regularly

11 A twelfth-century jug, found in London, imported from north-western Europe. (Museum of London)

changed and moneyers were obliged to pay a fee to the king or bishop for reminting. In 979 some fifty-three English towns minted their own coins. Moneyers could only work in towns and traders were forbidden to trade except in towns, but most mints were relatively modest in size and some appear to have been served by a single moneyer, with some moneyers serving more than one borough.

There was no immediate change in coin design after the Conquest, and Norman coins were often minted by Saxon moneyers, as at Oxford (see **2**). William and later Norman kings were careful to keep the English and Norman currencies separate. English coinage was melted down and reminted in Normandy, which is why very few Saxon or Anglo-Norman coins have been found in the Duchy, and few Norman coins have been uncovered in England. In 1107, a new coin, the halfpenny, was introduced and at Christmas 1124 there was a purge of moneyers, following repeated accusations of debased coinage and forgery. As many as 124 out of 150 English moneyers were punished by the loss of their right hand, castration and banishment. After this the Saxon system of periodic recoinage was abandoned and the national network of mints rationalized.

The Saxon countryside

Recent archaeological investigation has demonstrated that the intricate rural settlement pattern of late Saxon England was an amalgam of prehistoric, Roman, Saxon and Scandinavian elements. It is true that most of our current village-names are to be found for the first time within the folios of Domesday Book and therefore in a technical sense their history does not start until the coming of the Normans, although their origins in almost all cases were clearly of much greater antiquity. Domesday Book, however, is tantalizingly vague about the physical nature of the settlements it records, whether they were scattered hamlets or tightly nucleated villages, although a corpus of archaeological data relating to late Saxon rural settlement is now emerging. During the later Saxon period there was a gradual coalescence of rural settlement from isolated farmsteads and hamlets to nucleated villages. This was associated with an increasingly centralized secular and ecclesiastical administration and a rising population, trends that were to continue and accelerate after the Conquest. It is also clear that where nucleated villages did exist before 1066, they were on the whole smaller than they became during the twelfth and thirteenth centuries, when it is possible to measure their dimensions both from documentary evidence and from more extensive archaeological data.

Relatively few late Saxon village buildings have been excavated, and often it is not possible to determine which side of the Conquest some rural dwellings date from. The sunken-floored building, which was an important element in early Saxon settlement, had a remarkable resilience and continued to be used, normally in an ancillary role, well into the eleventh century. An urban example of this late date was discovered under the motte of Oxford Castle. More common are hall-houses of the type found at Sulgrave (Northants) and Goltho (Lincs.), where they have been interpreted as high-status thegns' houses – the equivalent of the post-Conquest manor house. Some of these appear to have been defended by a simple bank and ditch. There was probably a link between the location of churches and such late-Saxon fortified enclosures, but so few have been identified that there remain many unanswered questions about their nature and distribution, questions which can only be resolved by further fieldwork and excavation.

By 1086 much of the potentially good agricultural land appears to have been under cultivation; pockets of marsh and moor survived throughout the country until the post-medieval period, some of which were deliberately preserved, providing common rights for grazing and gathering or as Royal Forests. There were no large expanses of wilderness available for systematic colonization as were still to be found in parts of continental Europe, although the northern counties were relatively empty. Perhaps the nearest to this wilderness in England was created by the Normans as a consequence of the suppression of the English rebellion known as the 'Harrying of the North', which resulted in a large expanse of devastated land in the Midlands and the North in the late eleventh century. In Domesday Book such land was recorded as 'waste', i.e. land that had gone out of cultivation principally as a result of deliberate devastation. In addition to the waste caused by William's armies considerable disruption had been caused before the Conquest by internal rebellion and Welsh and Scottish raids. The Domesday folios of Cheshire, Shropshire and Herefordshire show that many villages already lay waste in 1066 as a result of the conflict between the Mercians and the Welsh. In the account for eleven settlements on the Herefordshire–Radnorshire border, the scene of a frontier incident three decades earlier, Domesday records that 'on these waste lands woods have grown up in which the said Osbern has the hunting and takes away what he can. Nothing else'.

Most elements of the medieval agricultural system appear to have been in place before the Conquest. The Normans were not directly responsible for any major agrarian changes, although during the eleventh century a heavier plough, using more iron components, was imported from France into England. There is still much discussion about when the open- or common-field system, found over much of England by the early thirteenth century, began. Under this system land was held in strips in large unfenced arable fields. Was this system fully established when the Normans arrived, or was it in the process of evolving, or was it a post-Norman development? Such archaeological evidence as there is indicates the existence of strip fields in the pre-Norman period, and yet the documentary evidence points towards the evolution of the mature open-field system during the twelfth and thirteenth centuries. It

seems probable that much arable was cultivated in strips at the time of the Norman Conquest, but in the wake of the Conquest the system was extended considerably.

The Domesday survey suggests that there were more sheep than all other livestock put together. At this point, the use of sheep was to provide milk to make cheese for winter food. Wool, manure and meat were by-products in order of importance. Some districts were already clearly dedicated to sheep farming, and in Essex and East Anglia, for example, there appear to have been broad belts of sheep pasture occupying land parallel to the coastline. Horses were important as a means of transport, but surviving equine equipment suggests that late Saxon horses were scarcely larger than ponies. The Norman use of cavalry at Hastings is seen as a major contributory factor in King Harold's defeat, and it seems probable that horses were not bred for fighting in England as they were in parts in Normandy, where they were reared in specialist parks.

Domesday Book suggests a countryside that was still fairly heavily wooded and where colonization was still taking place. References to *assarts*, i.e. land recently cleared for arable, have in the past been regarded as only hinting at the scale of reclamation taking place in the eleventh century. This assumption has recently been questioned and it is now apparent that far from being heavily forested, eleventh-century England was relatively open and that perhaps as little as 15 per cent of the countryside was wooded. Timber resources were already being carefully managed. Certain forms of timber were already rare before the Norman Conquest, and tall straight oaks required for shipbuilding, for example, grown in dense forest conditions appear to have been unobtainable in England even before 1066.

Domesday Book provides evidence of a range of rural activities, such as fisheries, watermills and vineyards. Most industry was also of a rural nature; for example, the record for Gloucester includes 'iron rods for making nails

12 Aerial photograph showing the pock-marked landscape of stone-quarrying at Barnack (Northants). Barnack limestone was used extensively in eastern England and East Anglia during the late Saxon and Norman period, but documentary references to the stone industry are rare. Domesday Book only makes passing reference to such industrial activities. (Cambridge University Collection of Air Photographs)

for the King's ships', but it is most likely that this referred to ironmaking in the Forest of Dean. Furnaces have been excavated at West Runton (Norfolk); Stamford (Lincs.); and Lyvedon (Northants), and leadworking was recorded in the Peak District of Derbyshire. Nevertheless, Domesday is silent about a broad range of industrial activity, including stone quarrying (**12**). The archaeological record, particularly in towns, is doing much to rectify our lack of knowledge of these everyday activities. Recently excavated artefacts from places such as London, York, Lincoln and Southampton are providing detailed evidence of living conditions and of local and regional trading patterns in late Saxon England.

Salt

Salt was a vital commodity in both pre- and post-Conquest England. In addition to flavouring and preserving food, salt was an essential element in butter and cheese manufacture (**13**). Fish, mainly in the form of herring, were caught in large quantities, salted within twenty-four hours and then moved about the country. Salt also had wide domestic and liturgical uses, as well as being an important ingredient in some industrial processes. Salt manufacture is one industry on which the information is relatively abundant. The chief areas of production of maritime salt were along the marshes and estuaries of the south and east coasts. Domesday Book includes a record of the number of salt pans on certain estates, sometimes also including a rent, either in money, fish or loads of salt. Caistor by Norwich, for example, had 45 salt pans and at Lynn (Dorset), some 27 saltworkers are recorded. The mounds of debris thrown up as a result of saltworking can be found along the coastline of eastern England and constitute the 'Fittes' of Lincolnshire and the 'Red Hills' of Exeter. In Lincolnshire such mounds can rise up to 7m (23ft) in height and 20m (66ft) in diameter. Analysis of the old coastline between Wisbech and King's Lynn (Norfolk) has shown that the location of a line of villages coincides with extensive areas of saltworking mounds. Furthermore, the parish churches at West Walton, Terrington St Clement and Clenchwarton stand on low mounds, and the irregular ground around St Margaret's Church

at King's Lynn appears to have been created as a result of saltworking; almost certainly these remnants of the saltworking industry pre-date the Conquest.

The inland centres of production were in Worcestershire and Cheshire, and were based on natural brine springs. Numerous pits and salt pans are recorded at Droitwich and Nantwich, and archaeological investigation has provided evidence of 'wich' (saltmaking) houses incorporating clay and timber-lined rectangular troughs within a wattle superstructure. Although these date to the twelfth century and later, they display building traditions which appear to have started as early as the ninth century, and while there is little written evidence of the process of manufacture, leaden pans for vat furnaces are recorded and occasionally we

13 The Domesday record of salt pans in Norfolk. (Norfolk Museums Service)

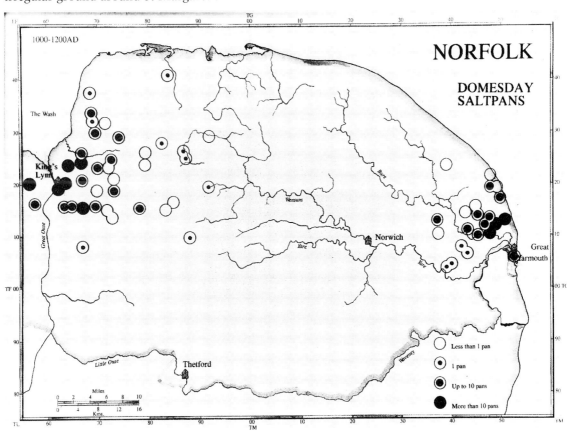

hear of wood for the salt pans. References to the Droitwich saltworks are found in several other Midland counties, reflecting the long-distance trade in salt which was carried along the routes known as 'Saltways'.

The Saxon Church

Architectural and archaeological evidence clearly shows that there were many more churches in late Saxon England than appear in the Domesday survey and that despite the extensive rebuilding that occurred after the Conquest several hundred churches incorporating Saxon architectural features survive today. In Norfolk, for example, Domesday Book records only 250 churches excluding Norwich, but it is clear from documentary and archaeological evidence that there were as many as 650, that is one for almost every parish in the county at that date. The building of a church was as much a demonstration of wealth and status as religious devotion, and the large number of Saxon churches in relatively prosperous areas such as East Anglia reflected the competitive spirit of late Saxon society, where status symbols mattered to landowners almost as much as to their Norman successors.

There are few surviving examples of early Saxon churches in England, largely because of later rebuilding. By the eleventh century the plans of English churches were already becoming more European in design. The side chapels or *porticos* gradually grew larger, becoming more like regular crosswings (transepts), in churches such as Brenmore (Hants) (*c.* 1010) and St Mary in Castro, Dover (*c.* 1020) and reaching a full cruciform plan with large crossing arches at the cathedral-like church of Stow (Lincs.) (1010–40) (**14**). The church bell-tower first came to England about 1000 through France from Italy, following the same route that Romanesque architecture was to take half a century later. The simplest of these towers were stocky and square with small windows and larger bell-openings near the top,

each having a double opening with a squat column in the centre. Hundreds of such towers survive in England, their Saxon elements often difficult to detect, as their bell-openings were later widened. Although Norman architecture made its appearance in England before the Conquest at Westminster Abbey (**15**), there is little evidence for Norman Romanesque elsewhere in England prior to 1066 (**colour plate 3**).

Decorative art in churches in England owed much to native tradition. Canterbury and Winchester had a long tradition of illuminated manuscripts which in turn influenced the style of post-Conquest sculpture. Anglo-Saxon manuscripts were much admired on the Continent for their vibrant colours and expressive vigorous style. Late Saxon manuscript illumination was itself based ultimately on Carolingian models. Saxon draughtsmen had absorbed this style and elaborated on it, making it their own. With it they produced fine line or wash drawings and illuminations rich in pinks and blues with a lavish use of gold. Another characteristic of these paintings was the profuse use of exuberant acanthus foliage painted in elaborate interwoven border patterns around full-page illuminations. The style was dominant in southern England at Glastonbury, Canterbury, Winchester, Ely and Ramsey, and is generically known as the Winchester school style. This in turn had a strong influence on Norman painting and to a lesser degree on sculpture (**colour plate 2**).

During the reign of Edward the Confessor, the Church maintained some of the energy generated by the monastic reform movement of the tenth century. Before the Conquest there were only thirty-five monasteries and nine nunneries south of the River Humber; a few of them were in a state of decay, but many were flourishing. Some of these were ancient establishments, such as Winchester and

14 The interior rounded crossing arch of the minster church at Stow (Lincs.), one of the largest surviving Saxon buildings in England. (National Monuments Record)

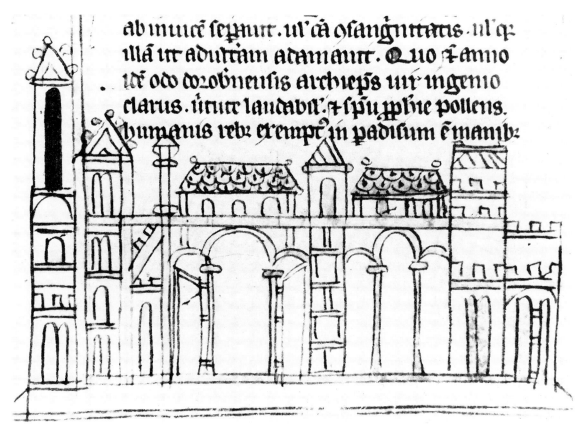

15 Edward the Confessor's Westminster Abbey church as shown in a thirteenth-century manuscript. The sketch shows the rounded arches and the western towers as still surviving at Jumièges (see **5**). (British Library)

Abingdon, but there was also a new generation of monasteries at places such as Cerne, Eynsham and Abbotsbury. Peterborough Abbey was wealthy, and in retrospect the decades prior to the Conquest were seen as a golden age. Other Anglo-Scandinavian kings had been responsible for the foundation of abbeys. Cnut had founded Bury St Edmunds and Harold, before he became king, established a community of secular canons at Waltham, a place of particular sanctity to the Saxons where he was eventually buried.

Many of the Saxon monasteries were wealthy with large estates and acquired a reputation (at least according to Norman sources) of having an easy-going, affluent lifestyle. The English monasteries housed aristocratic communities, and many of the abbots were from the nobility.

As cult centres of the old English saints they represented centres of nationalist sentiment after the Conquest and were broadly traditionalist in their interests. Although the liturgical regime was determined by the *Regularis Concordia*, a body of common usages agreed by English abbots and abbesses in 970 and modelled on Flemish practice, the English monasteries displayed little of the spiritual dynamism that characterized the Norman Church in the mid-eleventh century. It is arguable, however, that in terms of artistic achievement, particularly internal decoration and illuminated manuscripts, they surpassed their Norman counterparts.

In addition to the surviving standing Saxon structures, excavation has revealed pre-Conquest churches in several places. A few of these have been found within a rural context, for instance at the deserted village of Wharram Percy (Yorks.), but most of them are in towns. In some cases it is possible to trace the development from a wooden to a stone church, as at St Mark's, on the west side of Lincoln High Street. The church and its graveyard were probably established in the mid-tenth century in the form of a small rectangular timber building south of the later medieval church. In the mid-eleventh century a new church of stone was built next to the timber church, reusing masonry from local Roman buildings for its fabric. Most people were buried without a coffin in an unmarked grave close to the church. Investigation of early graveyards indicates that burial of laity inside the churches was not allowed until the twelfth century.

Many medieval town churches began life as chapels linked to private residences in the tenth or eleventh centuries, and this often determined their location, which tended to be set back from the main thoroughfare. Archaeological evidence has demonstrated that Winchester parish churches were being extended as early as the eleventh century, and it would appear that this increase in church size represents a change or extension from a private chapel to a wider and more public parochial function. Those towns which developed after the Conquest often have only one parish church, which initially had been built to serve a rural community. Where the new town was grafted on to an existing village, these churches are often not integrated into the town plan, but located some way from the medieval urban nucleus, located on their original site at the centre of the late Saxon nucleus, as at Thame in Oxfordshire (**16**). In the case of completely new post-Conquest towns, the parish church will form an integral part of the urban plan.

The politics of late Saxon England

The events of 1066 have tended to overshadow another conquest of England which had taken place earlier in the eleventh century. Cnut, the King of Denmark, who defeated the Saxons and became King of England in 1016, was one of four Danish monarchs to rule the whole or parts of England before the Norman Conquest. The early stages of Cnut's reign were marked by

reprisals against the English, including a large number of executions and massacres – there was a particularly brutal one at Christmas 1017, after which surviving pretenders to the throne were pursued to exile or death. After Cnut had married Ethelred II's widow, Emma of Normandy, he began to assimilate Englishmen into his court and government and attempted with some success to create an Anglo-Scandinavian culture. Cnut built himself a reputation as a sponsor of trade and patron of the Church, founding monasteries and even making a pilgrimage to Rome in 1027. The English bishops remained in post and the reformed abbeys continued to flourish. Like William after him, Cnut seems to have used the government he inherited and did not make fundamental constitutional changes, although he did issue new law codes.

Cnut was responsible for dividing the kingdom into four parts, Northumbria, East Anglia, Mercia and Wessex, each under the rule of an earl. In 1020 he passed Wessex to an Englishman, Godwin, whose role in subsequent English politics was to be of profound significance. Godwin became the most powerful man in England after the king married a Danish princess, Gytha; it was their son, Harold, who was to assume the throne on the death of Edward the Confessor in 1066.

Edward the Confessor and the succession

To understand how Saxon England ended up under Norman control it is necessary to examine the early career of Edward the Confessor, a monarch who, although branded a 'holy simpleton' by some, was able to maintain his kingdom in a state of relative peace during a period of considerable political turbulence. Edward, born in 1003, was the son of Ethelred II and Emma. Following the normal practice with possible successors to the throne during the rule of Danish kings, Edward was exiled and attached to the Norman court. He was recalled to England in 1041 and succeeded his half-brother Harthacnut to the throne in the

16 Aerial view of Thame (Oxon.). The town plan is typical of many undefended new towns created in the two centuries after the Conquest. The cigar-shaped market place was designed to allow maximum space for trading but allowed access at both ends to be controlled by narrow entrances. (Cambridge University Collection of Air Photographs)

following year. When he became king he turned to his kinsmen in Normandy to join him as companions and administrators, and as he was childless he also looked to the Norman ducal family for a successor. Edward's reliance upon Normans proved increasingly unpopular in England, and many of them, including the Archbishop of Canterbury, Robert of Jumièges, were eventually forced to return to Normandy. Subsequently Edward relied heavily on Godwin, the Earl of Wessex, father of the later King Harold. There were several candidates to succeed Edward to the throne including Edgar the Atheling (prince), King Magnus of Norway, Harold's half-brother Tostig and of course Duke William of Normandy, to whom it is reported that Edward had promised the crown during his exile in Normandy.

2
The conquest of England

Duke William of Normandy

Duke William II of Normandy was born at
Falais, about 30km (19 miles) to the south of
Caen in 1027–8, the bastard son of Duke
Robert I or Robert the Magnificent. Robert died
while returning from pilgrimage to Jerusalem in
1035, and thus William succeeded to the
dukedom when he was only 8. His minority saw
a period close to anarchy in the Duchy during
which two of his guardians were assassinated.
William survived this troubled phase, and
formally came of age in 1044 when he was
almost immediately involved in an internal
revolt, which was not finally crushed until the
decisive battle of Val-ès-Dunes (1047), after
which he ruled with formidable skill. It is
recorded that William was a pious and an able
man but was also resourceful and ruthless.
These were attributes which do not make him
particularly attractive to us, but they were
characteristics which enabled him to dominate
first Normandy and then England (see p. 47).

William's long apprenticeship was to serve him
well when he definitively took the reins of power.
The strengthening of military feudalism was
accompanied by a general tightening of ducal
administration, providing William with the most
able army in Europe. As Duke of Normandy (and
indeed later as King of England) William exercised
firm control over his magnates, while building up
and training his military resources, and fighting
his enemies, both internal and external. He
embarked on a series of successful and brutal
campaigns which eventually brought the whole of
Maine under Norman control and subdued
Brittany, over which he claimed lordship. Thus by
1066 William had established himself as master of
north-west Gaul, and was a powerful European
sovereign in all but name (**17**).

William had also encouraged the centralization
of both secular and ecclesiastical power into
urban centres. In particular, he engineered the
development of Caen, where he created a fortress-
town which had access to the sea by the River

17 The seal of William the Conqueror, showing him
armed and mounted, a convention followed by later
Norman kings. (British Museum)

ENERVNT · AD DOL: ET CONAN: FVGA

18 Siege of the castle at Dol (Brittany) on the Bayeux Tapestry. The castle, depicted as a motte, is being besieged by Duke William's cavalry. On the right Count Conan is shown making his escape by rope from the burning wooden tower on top of the castle mound.

Orne, but was not as vulnerable as the ancient regional capital Rouen, which was more open to attack by way of the Seine valley. Caen also lies at the very heart of a narrow belt of Jurassic limestone, an excellent building material, which provided a major source of stone for the construction of the castles, churches and monasteries in Normandy and later England. By 1060 William had built a stone castle at Caen, traces of which have recently been identified. He was also responsible for constructing the two fine abbeys of Holy Trinity and St Stephen, which dominated the city and were constructed as part-penance for the uncanonical nature of William's marriage to Matilda, daughter of Baldwin V, Count of Flanders, in the early 1050s. Papal opposition to the marriage was only lifted in 1059 after Lanfranc interceded on behalf of William.

William's claim to the throne of England lay principally through his grand-aunt, Emma, and, according to Norman sources, a pledge made by Edward the Confessor. Reputedly, on leaving the Norman court in 1051, Edward the Confessor had promised William that he would succeed to the English throne on Edward's death. Again, according to the Norman version of the story

this promise was reinforced in 1064 or 1065 when he sent Harold, by then Earl of Wessex, to Normandy to confirm the commitment. Harold's journey is depicted in detail on the Bayeux Tapestry, where he is shown as a party to this arrangement. Furthermore, during his stay in France events conspired to make him William's bondsman. Having sailed from Bosham (Sussex), the ships taking Harold and his companions to France were blown off course and landed in Ponthieu to the north of Normandy. Here the English party was taken prisoner by Guy of Ponthieu and the ransom demanded for Harold's release was paid by William.

On arrival at the Norman court, Harold joined William on a military campaign during which he fought alongside but subservient to William in a number of battles against the Bretons, including the siege of two marcher castles at Dol and Dinan (**18**). Finally, just

19 (a) Nineteenth-century print of the ruins of the Norman ducal palace at Lillebonne, Normandy.
(b) Fécamp: the palace here has largely been destroyed, but excavations have recently uncovered the remains of the early Norman building.

before his return to England Harold is shown publicly swearing an oath of allegiance to William on holy relics. In the eyes of the Normans, such an oath served to underline William's legitimate claim to the English throne and to highlight the duplicity and treachery of Harold's subsequent actions. While on the English side of the Channel it seemed reasonable that the premier Saxon earl should take over the crown from the childless Edward, on the French side the Normans were in no doubt that the throne was rightfully William's. On hearing the news of Edward's death on 5 January 1066 and of Harold's accession on the same day, William summoned a Norman council at the ducal palace at Bonneville-sur-Touques (**19**), where the decision was made to assemble a force to invade England and take the English crown by military action. He also set about the necessary diplomatic preparations for secular and papal support for the invasion of England. In England Harold's hold on the crown was far from secure, and according to the Bayeux Tapestry the portents were not good; at the time of his coronation the tapestry portrays the appearance of Halley's Comet along with the ghostly outlines of the Norman invasion fleet (in fact the comet appeared later that year). Harold relied on a series of alliances in order to maintain order, and he strengthened his links with the brothers Edwin, Earl of Mercia, and Morcar, Earl of Northumbria, by marrying their sister, but such links were fragile, uneasily bringing into the royal circle established political figures whose loyalty to Harold remained lukewarm.

The events of 1066

After deciding on the invasion of England, William requisitioned those boats already in Norman harbours and then set about building a fleet of transport ships and mustering forces drawn from neighbouring French principalities with which he forged alliances; in particular he engaged the mercenary naval services of Flanders. There is a contemporary ship list, which details the contributions of the leading Norman magnates; William's half-brother Robert of Mortain provided 120 ships and his other half-brother Odo of Bayeux 100, while William Fitz Osbern, Hugh of Avranches, Roger of Montgomery and Roger of Beaumont provided 60 ships each. The Bayeux Tapestry, on which we have to rely for much of our detailed evidence for the invasion, records the meticulous care taken to provide the invasion force with an adequate supply of arms, horses and provisions as well as the actual construction of boats to carry the force across the Channel. William's fleet was assembled at Dives-sur-Mer, close to Caen, but early in August he moved it to St-Valery-sur-Somme in Ponthieu, from where he accurately judged he could sail directly into the heart of Harold's own territory in Sussex. There followed a long delay while William, according to some accounts, waited for favourable weather conditions, but more probably he had calculated that Harold's waiting forces would disintegrate after such a long interval.

While these events were unfolding there was another threat to Harold in the North. In May of that year his half-brother Tostig had made naval attacks on southern and eastern England, prompting the premature mobilization of the English army. Tostig was repulsed and moved north, but the English forces were then obliged to face a full summer under arms waiting for an attack from across the Channel. In early September the strain of such a long mobilization, plus a spell of stormy weather at sea, which suggested that there might not even be an invasion that year, persuaded Harold to disperse the army and send his fleet back to London.

In mid-September Tostig in alliance with Harold Hardrada attacked York. Harold III of Norway is one of the most interesting of eleventh-century figures and is often described as the last of the Viking chieftains. He had been wounded at the battle of Stiklestad (1030), in which his half-brother St Olaf was killed, but had escaped to serve in the Byzantine emperor's Varangian guard at Constantinople. He had then returned to contend successfully for the crown of Norway, where his strong rule earned him the sobriquet 'Hardrada' or 'hard counsel'. Initially the northern earls successfully contained the invaders at the battle of Gate Fullford, but they were eventually defeated with heavy losses. On hearing the news, Harold reassembled his army and marched swiftly northwards. On 25 September he surprised and overwhelmed the invaders at the battle of Stamford Bridge (20), where both Harold Hardrada and Tostig were killed. It was reported that of the 300 ships that had transported the Norwegian army to England only 25 were required to carry the survivors home. Stamford Bridge was a great victory for the English, and undoubtedly it is a battle which would have enjoyed a far higher historical profile had it not been for subsequent events in the South. Stamford Bridge was also the last significant hand-to-hand battle to be fought on English soil; the Norman use of cavalry and bowmen was to change the face of English warfare for ever.

20 The modern bridge over the River Derwent at Stamford Bridge (Yorks.). The site of the battle where King Harold defeated an invading army led by his half-brother Tostig and King Harold Hardrada of Norway a few weeks before the battle of Hastings.

On 27 September with a favourable wind behind it William's armada set sail while the English army was still in York (**21**). The following morning the fleet landed unopposed at the ancient fort of Pevensey in Sussex, the Roman Anderita, which had originally been built to defend the south coast against the Anglo-Saxons in the middle of the third century AD. The Roman fort enclosed an area of about 3ha (10 acres) and the original walls, still standing to a height of up to 6m (20ft) in places, were strengthened by a series of round towers. On landing, William reinforced the existing fortifications by narrowing the former Roman west gate with a wall in front of the guard-chambers and cutting away a curving ditch in front. The arch of the Roman east gate was also repaired and fighting platforms were added to two other towers. A pit containing a wooden ladder, a cask, bowls and four eleventh-century jugs from Normandy has been excavated in the outer bailey, and it is thought that these objects represent relics of the invading force. After the Conquest Pevensey was granted to Robert of Mortain, who founded a small borough outside the Roman fort, repairing the original walls and building a castle within it (**colour plate 4**).

After landing at Pevensey, William, still uncertain of the situation, needed to maintain close contact with his fleet. Therefore on 29 September he moved both his ships and his army eastwards to Hastings, where he was able to utilize the superior harbour facilities. According to one source Harold sent a fleet to blockade Hastings. It is recorded that William erected a fortification within the town, and this was almost certainly the castle which appears in the course of construction under his direction on the Bayeux Tapestry (see **7**). The much-eroded promontory castle at Hastings was investigated in the 1960s but failed to provide any definitive evidence of William's presence there. The excavations showed that the castle mound was built of alternating layers of sand and clay, and it has been suggested that the round bags slung around the shoulders of one of the castle's diggers depicted on the Bayeux Tapestry contained sand. While in Hastings William's army ravaged the surrounding countryside in

21 Bayeux Tapestry: the Norman army on the march conveying arms, stores and wine towards the invasion armada. Duke William is depicted just before he embarks. (BBC Hulton Picture Library)

order to obtain supplies and to intimidate the English; evidence of this harassment appears in the scene on the tapestry in which, before the battle of Hastings, Norman soldiers are portrayed as setting fire to a house from which a mother and child are making their escape.

The battle of Hastings

News of the Norman landing reached Harold after the battle of Stamford Bridge and the English troops marched swiftly southwards, reaching London by 6 October; just five days later Harold began to move his reinforced army towards the south coast. Before dusk on 13 October Duke William heard that the enemy was within striking distance of his base at Hastings, and early the following morning he moved his army northwards. Harold, confronted by the Normans, took up a defensive position along an escarpment known as 'the place of the grey apple tree' and to the Normans as 'Senlac' ('sandy lake'). Senlac Hill was the highest rise of ground between Hastings and the modern town of Battle. According to some sources the Normans, 'eager for battle', started to attack the Saxons well before their army was fully in position. Numerically the armies appear to have been well matched. Harold is thought to have had 6000 or 7000 men, although it is not known what the balance was between trained fighting men, thegns, housecarls and peasant militia. Duke William's army is thought to have consisted of some 2000 knights with 4000–5000 support troops, infantry, archers and crossbow men (**22**).

Much has been written about the battle of Hastings, its tactics, and the relative qualities of the English and Norman troops and their commanders, but some aspects of this decisive conflict inevitably remain unclear. It appears that the Norman strategy was to sustain attacks up the short, steep incline to the summit of the hill on which Harold was based. Their archers were able to weaken the English army, but in order to win it was necessary to penetrate Harold's ranks and destroy the elite forces in

close combat. For much of the day the English repulsed the Norman attacks, and at times the Normans fell back in considerable confusion. At one point the rumour spread that Duke William had been killed, and the Bayeux Tapestry shows him lifting his helmet to show his face and thus reassure his troops. The tapestry also portrays a number of Norman knights breaking through the English lines and the death of Harold's brothers, Leofwine and Gyrth, long before the closing stages of the battle. As the day wore on the Normans began to gain the advantage, partly by employing the tactic of the 'feigned flight', in which Norman contingents retreated in apparent confusion, tempting groups of English to pursue them down the hill. Careful drilling made it possible for the Norman cavalry then to turn in good order and charge down the pursuing English infantry (**colour plate 5**).

Eventually the Normans penetrated through to the heart of the English command, where Harold still stood behind a wall of shields with his dragon standard. The scene is vividly portrayed on the Bayeux Tapestry; the standard was thrown down, the king's bodyguard was slaughtered, and Harold, wounded but still fighting, was cut down by a Norman knight. The Bayeux Tapestry also shows Harold with an arrow through his eye. It is the only source of this story, and scholars believe that the tapestry was using a convention – in fact an invention to underline the central theme of the tapestry – God punishing the English and Harold in particular for his perjury. The Normans saw their success at the battle of Hastings as a vindication of William's rightful claims to be the lawful successor to Edward the Confessor. Harold had received retribution as a disloyal vassal and was rightly overthrown.

Those English troops who survived sought cover in the country to the north at dusk. Some of them turned in acts of final defiance to inflict further losses on their Norman enemies; in an incident known as 'the Malfosse' many Norman cavalry perished after they were led into a concealed ditch. Norman chroniclers noted with

22 The Temple pyx, showing fully armed Norman soldiers sleeping. (The Burrell Collection, Glasgow Museum)

pride that some of the most famous Norman fighters of their day died at Hastings, but it was the English who had lost their king and most of their nobility. One authority has described the battle as a 'conflict between the military methods of the seventh century and those of the eleventh century'. It was the major and final act in the death of the Anglo-Scandinavian military tradition.

Many of the details of military dress and weaponry shown on the Bayeux Tapestry have been confirmed by archaeological finds of contemporary date found throughout western Europe and Scandinavia. However, no systematic archaeological examination of the battlefield has taken place and artefacts from the battle have been found randomly; for example, a throwing axe or *francisca* almost certainly used in the battle was found there earlier this century. Within a few years Battle Abbey was built on the site of the victory, according to tradition with the high altar located on the spot where Harold had died; it was in fact an extremely inconvenient location for such a foundation (**23**). The site lies on a narrow ridge on open heathland and in order to build the abbey it was necessary to undertake extensive terracing and the construction of massive undercrofts. Convention states that William built Battle Abbey to fulfil a vow to build a monastery if he was victorious. It is more likely that the construction of the abbey was part of an arrangement made between the pope and King William in about 1070, when William was recognized by papal legates, but simultaneously suffered heavy penalties for the excessive bloodshed involved in the conquest of England.

Although the eastern arm of Battle Abbey church was sufficiently complete to allow for its consecration in 1076, it was not until 1094 that the finished church was finally consecrated in the presence of William II, the Archbishop of Canterbury and seven bishops. On his death the Conqueror bequeathed to the community at Battle his royal cloak, a collection of relics and a portable altar used during his military campaigns. He had also endowed the abbey with extensive estates including all the land within a one-and-a-half-mile (2.5km) radius of the high altar. Within this area the abbot enjoyed supreme jurisdiction over land and men. This gift promoted Battle to the rank of fifteenth wealthiest religious house in England.

William's journey to London

The battle of Hastings was decisive, but it was only the beginning of the Norman conquest of England. This took several years to accomplish fully, and, although there was no other confrontation of equal scale and ferocity between the Normans and the English, Norman control in many areas was only imposed by determined, and frequently brutal, means. The English were still capable of raising an opposing army, and despite the massacre of many English magnates at Hastings a number of pretenders to the throne survived. William was cautious about besieging London immediately and adopted a policy of intimidation and persuasion in southern England. After his victory, William returned to Hastings in order to rest the victorious army for about a week and to allow time for the surrender of the surviving English earls, but no such submissions were made. According to William of Poitiers, William the Conqueror's chaplain, on Friday 20 October William 'left Hastings in charge of a brave commander and proceeded to New Romney, where he punished at his pleasure those who had previously killed some of his men after a struggle'; this action was apparently a reprisal for an attack by the English on some of his foraging troops. The Bayeux Tapestry in its present form ends with Harold's death and the English troops fleeing from the battlefield in disarray, but the tapestry is incomplete and the missing section almost certainly portrayed William's triumphal march to London, culminating in his coronation there.

The story can be reconstructed of William and his army to London on a circuitous route through southern England, a journey which in

23 Battle Abbey (Sussex) from the air. The abbey was founded by William on the site of the battle of Hastings, with the high altar of the church located on the spot where King Harold was killed. The town, which lies outside the gatehouse, was planned soon after the abbey was founded in the late eleventh century. (Cambridge University Collection of Air Photographs)

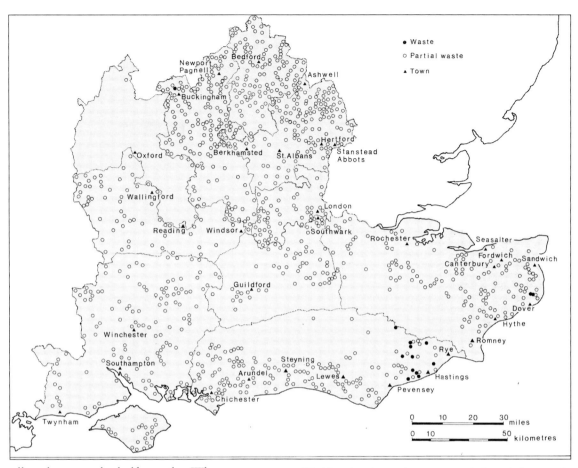

24 Map showing settlements recorded as wholly or partly devastated in 1070. The lines of 'waste' manors demarcate the movement of William's armies after the Conquest. (Judith Dobie)

all took two and a half months. Wherever possible William utilized the surviving Roman road system, for although some sections had fallen out of use, it would appear from the route which he took in south-east England that the network was still largely intact. The chronicler monk John of Worcester (died 1141) recounts that in the course of his march William 'laid waste' Sussex, Kent, Hampshire, Surrey, Middlesex and Hertfordshire. The Norman army lived off the land during the Conquest, and the progress of the troops can be mapped through the entries in Domesday Book. The march of the invaders from Hastings to London and then in a wide circle around London had a spectacular impact on the towns and villages through which they passed and from whose inhabitants they took cattle, corn and other provisions. So great was the damage caused that twenty years later it was still reflected in the reduced values of those places along the line of the march (**24**). The various risings against the Normans were ruthlessly suppressed and punished by Norman armies with a ferocity designed to deter further resistance, and such actions also left scars on the countryside which were a long time in the healing.

Apparently, the brutality of William's response at Romney persuaded the inhabitants of Dover to surrender on the following day; William then moved his army to the town. According to some sources, it is there that William and his troops contracted dysentery. Disease was a constant threat to large armies billeted in confined quarters; in addition to the problems of human sanitation, there were hundreds of tons of horse manure to cope with, posing a serious risk to health. The Normans occupied the site of an Iron Age promontory fort at Dover, which had been reinforced by the Romans and the Saxons and which would still have had extensive walls surviving in 1066. William of Poitiers notes: 'This castle is situated on a rock adjoining the sea and is raised up by nature and so strongly fortified that it stands like a straight wall as high as an arrow's flight. Its side is washed by the sea. While its inhabitants were preparing to surrender unconditionally our men greedy for booty set fire to the castle, and the greater part of it was soon enveloped in flames' (**25**). It is further recorded that William spent eight days here improving the fortifications, but the only known excavated evidence for William's siegeworks here are in the form of a 5.5m (18ft) deep ditch which cut across the Saxon cemetery of St Mary in Castro.

Close to Dover, William met representatives from Canterbury, the ecclesiastical capital of England, who offered him the city's surrender on 29 October. It is not known if William spent much time in the metropolitan city, but it appears that as at Pevensey and Dover he reused the Roman defences, and fortified a Roman burial mound to create a castle. Excavations in Dane John gardens (Norman Donjon) have identified a 3m (10ft) deep ditch, which was backfilled in the late twelfth century; the contents of the ditch contained waterlogged timber, which may have originated from the original Norman bailey palisade. The site of the castle was moved further round the circuit of Roman town walls in the early twelfth century. At this stage William's men appear to have been so badly affected by dysentery that they were forced to delay for nearly a month at a place called 'the broken tower', which may have been the Roman fortress at Richborough near Sandwich. When they resumed their journey towards London, William and his men followed the line of the Roman Watling Street, which starts at Dover and runs through Faversham to

Rochester. From Faversham onwards, his route lay relatively close to the Thames estuary, so that the Norman soldiers may have been able to maintain some contact with their fleet, which could have been used to carry supplies for an army still uncertain of its eventual fate.

At about this time, William was met by a deputation from Edward the Confessor's widow, Edith, and the dowager queen offered up Winchester, the ancient capital of Wessex, to William; this was an important acquisition as the royal treasury was housed there and, after London, Winchester was the most important urban centre in southern England. The city did not lie on William's direct route, but it is possible that it was occupied by a second Norman army, which may have landed at Southampton and marched northwards to meet the main body of William's troops. By this stage William controlled much of south-eastern England, but London remained unconquered. He therefore proceeded northwards and camped at Southwark on the southern side of the Thames from London. An English army, under the nominal control of Edgar the Atheling, who had been proclaimed king by the surviving rebellious English, occupied the capital and some of his troops made a sortie across the river into Southwark, where the Normans drove them back across the bridge and then burnt all the buildings south of the river.

Despite the chronicler's rhetoric, which insisted that William had 'dealt a double blow to the pride of his stubborn foes', it seems inconceivable that William would have missed this opportunity of occupying London had he been capable of doing so. Instead he moved his army westwards; the precise route he took is uncertain, but it is probable that he passed through the important royal centres of Windsor and Reading on his way to Wallingford, a major Saxon *burh* and river crossing (see **9**). The taking of Wallingford effectively sealed off the middle Thames from any uprising. There were already considerable fortifications around the town, but a large motte and bailey castle was

25 (a) The Norman keep at Dover Castle. (English Heritage)
(b) The Norman chapel interior (National Monuments Record/Batsford)
(c) The Norman chapel. (English Heritage)

26 An extract from the account of the battle of Hastings from the Anglo-Saxon Chronicle. (British Library)

erected by the Normans in the south-eastern quadrant of the Saxon settlement. While the Norman army was at Wallingford, Stigand, the Archbishop of Canterbury, finally transferred his allegiance to William.

The Normans then turned eastwards and moved along the foot of the Chilterns, eventually encamping at Berkhamsted, where the surviving English leaders submitted to William and offered him the throne: 'William was met by Archbishop Ealdred [Archbishop of York], Edgar the Atheling, Earl Edwin and Earl Morcar and all the chief men of London, who submitted from force of circumstances, but only when the depredation was complete. It was great folly that they had not done sooner', mused the gloomy Anglo-Saxon chronicler. 'But God would not remedy matters because of our sins. They gave him hostages and swore oaths of fealty, and he promised to be a gracious liege lord' (**26**). There is some question whether it was at Great or Little Berkhamsted that the surrender took place, but the presence of a formidable motte and bailey castle at Great Berkhamsted, which was given to Robert of Mortain and remained in royal hands throughout much of the Middle Ages, along with circumstantial geographical evidence, suggests that it was here that the Londoners submitted to the inevitable (**27**).

William's coronation

William eventually entered London with little opposition, although there appears to have been a skirmish with the citizens near the Roman city walls just before Christmas. Arrangements were immediately made for his coronation and he was crowned by the Archbishop of York on Christmas Day 1066 in Westminster Abbey next to Edward the Confessor's tomb. However, even this momentous event did not pass without incident; during the service, Norman soldiers outside the abbey appear to have misunderstood the shouts which marked the acclamation and, thinking a riot had started, set fire to the neighbouring houses. William's coronation marked the end of 'legitimate war', and after this, in theory at least, only English rebels were denied royal protection. After his coronation William moved his army to Barking and completed his encirclement of London. Here he summoned a further meeting with English magnates from whom he demanded submission and recognition and to whom in return he again gave a pledge of fair government.

Planning, military skill and perhaps a little good luck had enabled William to win at Hastings and gain London, but to complete the conquest and establish firm foundations for his

rule it was essential to keep a substantial part of his army on a war footing. Immediately after his coronation William began to build a castle in order to control the capital, and this was constructed in the south-east corner of the Roman wall enclosing the city of London. Twelve years later the Normans, who had become weary of 'the fickleness of the vast and fierce population of London', began work on a great stone keep to improve the temporary fortifications of 1067. This was the White Tower, so called because its masonry was once coated with whitewash, which still stands complete at the centre of a complex of towered walls, baileys, domestic buildings and outworks added by later kings. Gundulph, the Norman Bishop of Rochester, 'a man very competent and skilful at building in stone', was the designer who raised for William a massive fortified palace, complete with great hall and chapel, roughly 30m (98ft) square and 26m (85ft) high. Its walls, 4.5m (15ft) thick at their base, were proof against all known ballistic devices of the time. In its original form it was probably not finished until the end of the eleventh century, and William would not have seen the completed building (**28**). The Conqueror constructed two other castles in the vicinity of London at Mont Fitchet, near Ludgate, and Baynard's Castle on the Thames near St Paul's Cathedral, but little above-ground evidence of these fortifications survives.

Although William had yet to complete the conquest of the country, in March 1067 he felt confident enough to return to Normandy, leaving England in the charge of two of his most trusted Norman magnates. William Fitz Osbern, his steward, was established at Winchester, while Bishop Odo of Bayeux was entrusted with Dover and the Kentish ports in order to maintain communication with Normandy. Having made these arrangements the king took with him as hostages a group of important Englishmen, including Edgar the Atheling, the Earls Edwin and Morcar and Archbishop Stigand. They sailed from where the successful Norman invading fleet

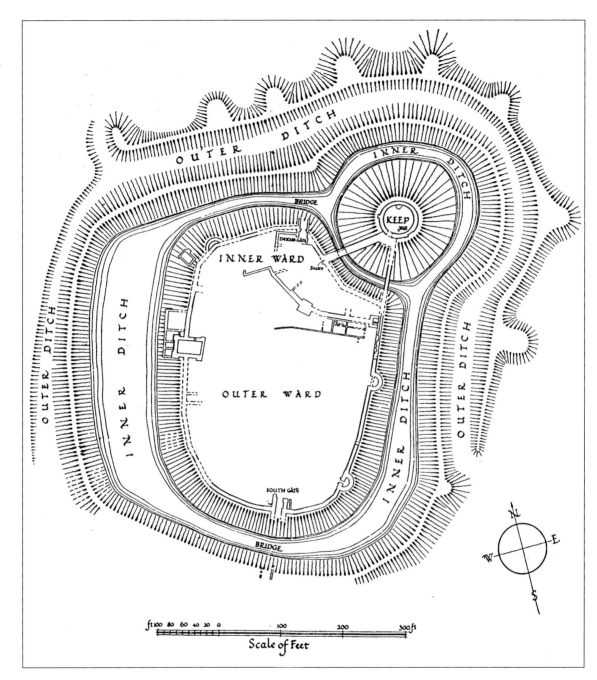

27 The plan of Berkhamsted Castle, showing the motte and bailey, which was subsequently reinforced, and remained in use until the Civil War in the seventeenth century. The surviving English forces eventually surrendered to William here after the battle of Hastings. The original castle was almost certainly built by William's half-brother, Robert, Count of Mortain. A subsequent holder was Thomas Becket, when he was Chancellor of England between 1155 and 1165. It seems probable that the oldest surviving masonry dates from his time. (English Heritage)

28 Aerial view of the Tower of London, with the White Tower at the centre of a series of outer defensive circuits. The Tower was William's great citadel and palace in the capital. As originally built (c. 1078), the castle consisted of the keep with a bailey running down to the Thames in the south-east angle of the Roman city wall. The Tower was amongst the largest structures of its kind in medieval Europe and the Romanesque arcading of the second-floor exterior extravagantly distinguishes the upper palatial accommodation from the largely defensive lower floor. The White Tower was eventually incorporated as the central feature of a much larger castle, the whole of which is known as the Tower of London. (Aerofilms)

had landed, Pevensey, and while in Normandy participated in elaborate celebrations at Rouen and Fécamp marking the conquest of England. An unsuccessful attack on Dover by Eustace of Boulogne, one of his allies at Hastings, persuaded William to return to England in December 1067. He celebrated Easter 1068 at Winchester, and at Whitsuntide, his wife, Matilda, was solemnly crowned as Queen of England at Winchester, but the Conquest was far from over: in fact he had only conquered Wessex, and the task of bringing the rest of England under Norman control was unfinished business.

3
The imposition of Norman rule

Once crowned King of England, William needed to reward his Norman supporters but at the same time to come to terms with the surviving English magnates and weld together Norman and English elements in his court, Church and administration. To begin with William showed tolerance to the defeated English. Edgar the Atheling was treated as a kinsman and 'endowed with wide lands', which he lost only when he subsequently rebelled against the king. Among the English churchmen who served him, Ealdred, Archbishop of York, was loyal until his death in 1069 and Wulfstan, Bishop of Worcester, was a valuable supporter both of the Conqueror and of his son, William Rufus. Other English bishops continued to appear at the royal court until 1070. Those Englishmen who submitted to William had their land and offices confirmed and were taken under his protection. However, these favours were not given without cost; for example, the monks of Peterborough had to pay the king 40 gold marks to redeem their estates, and similar sums were paid by other abbeys and individuals. This money accounts in part for the wealth that William was able to take across to Normandy in 1067.

Despite the initial tolerance of those English who co-operated with William, great areas of land were confiscated from those who had opposed him, notably Harold's estates in Wessex. Monastic estates were expropriated and typically William ordered Baldwin, Abbot of Bury St Edmunds, to hand over the land of his tenants who had fought against the king and died at the battle of Hastings; for their families the future was bleak. Elsewhere land in politically sensitive areas such as the Welsh Marches was also seized and given to William's men.

The English Revolt

William's attitude to the English altered markedly between 1067 and 1070 when there were a series of uprisings – at Exeter, at Dover, in the Midlands, along the Welsh Marches, in East Anglia and in the North. Vigorous campaigning under William's leadership gave the Normans the advantage until 1069, when they had control of the South-East and were making considerable progress in the South-West. Even at this stage there was a degree of co-operation: for instance, when William attacked Exeter in 1067 there were Englishmen in his forces. Significantly, too, it was the English who repulsed King Harold's sons when they attempted to land with forces in the South-West. The Midlands were partially subdued and the first steps were taken to stabilize and hold the frontier between England and Wales, but beyond the Humber Norman power rested on uneasily held bases. York, the capital of the North, was a danger point, politically and strategically too important to neglect, while further north there was hostile territory still to be subdued, with Durham conspicuous as a remote and isolated Norman outpost (**29**).

When William returned to England in 1067 he brought with him more Norman clerics and barons. His regent in Normandy, Roger of Montgomery, was installed at Arundel, adjacent to Humphrey of Tilleul at Hastings and William Warenne at Lewes. Pevensey was already in the hands of Robert of Mortain. These four castles dominated the Sussex rapes named after them; the fifth rape, Bramber, held by William of Braose, was created later. The rapes of Sussex were effectively 'castleries' on the continental model and superseded former administrative units; a similar structure of castleries may have been planned for Kent under Odo, Bishop of Bayeux, but was not implemented (30). This administrative rearrangement was not replicated elsewhere in England, where the Saxon system of local government was for the most part retained.

29 Aerial view of Durham, showing the cathedral lying in the centre of the island defined by the River Wear. The castle lies to the right of the cathedral. (National Monuments Record)

Early in 1068 King Harold's mother, Gytha, led another uprising at Exeter. The city was besieged for eighteen days and after its fall there was fresh Norman settlement in western Wessex. Norman magnates moved into the South-West; at Exeter the Castle of Rougemont was built and given to Baldwin of Meulles, and Robert of Mortain built a castle at Montacute (Som.). The siege of Exeter and its aftermath marked the turning point in the relationship between the English and the Normans. The policy of coexistence turned to one of domination.

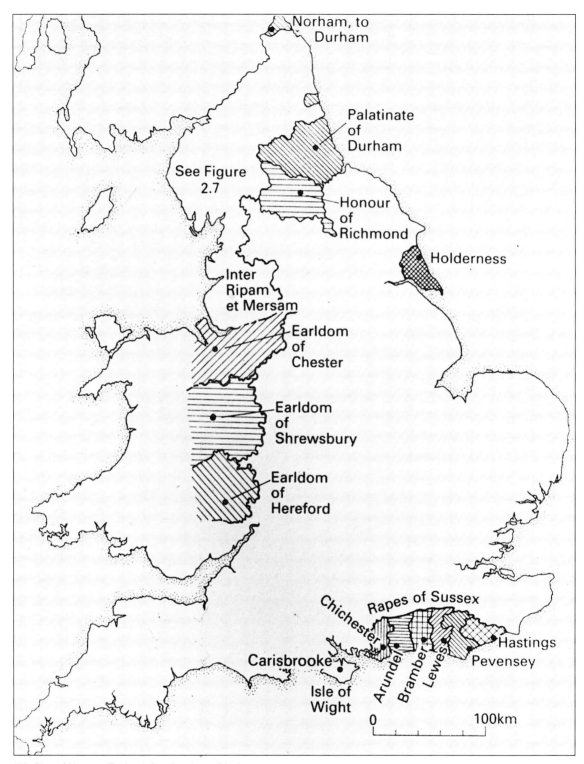

30 Plan of Norman England showing the political arrangements for the border regions including the Sussex rapes, which were 'castleries' based on the pattern found in France.

In May 1068, following the imposition of new taxation levies, the English Earls Edwin and Morcar turned against William, and the focus of his attention was transferred to the Welsh Marches and the North. Roger of Montgomery was appointed Earl of Shrewsbury, where he constructed a castle at the neck of the loop of the River Severn, which encircled the Saxon town. The chronicler Orderic Vitalis described an alliance of the English with the Welsh prince Bleddyn of Gwynedd as a signal for a general insurrection against Norman rule. But the real problem was in the North. Following no response to a demand for the submission of the English Northumbrian magnates, the king marched upon them in force, firstly to Warwick, and then Nottingham; work on castle construction began immediately in both county towns. The building of Nottingham Castle appears to have thrown the people of York into a panic, and they sent William the city keys and hostages. William entered York unopposed and built the first castle on the site of the later Clifford's Tower (31). These decisive moves brought much of the North, temporarily at least, under William's control. He then moved southwards to Lincoln, Huntingdon and Cambridge, where further castles were built and more hostages taken.

31 Clifford's Tower, York, a late twelfth-century stone keep sitting on top of the earlier Norman motte. (National Monuments Record)

By the autumn of 1068 William once more felt secure enough to return to Normandy and a number of Normans returned home with him, abandoning their English lands in the process. He appointed Robert Comins as Earl of Northumbria, with responsibility for control in the North. Robert was described by Simeon of Durham as 'one of those persons who paid the wages of their followers by licensing their ravages and murders'. On his arrival in the North in December 1068 he allowed his men to plunder, but in January 1069 the Northumbrians broke into the city of Durham and killed the Norman contingent, including Robert. The Northumbrians themselves erected a castle at Durham and made various attacks on the Normans, and at about the same time a rebel army under the leadership of Edgar the Atheling took York, except the castle, which remained in Norman hands. William returned from Normandy and moved north with a speed rivalling that of Harold's march to York in 1066, and like Harold before him, he 'came upon them by surprise from the south with an overwhelming army and routed them and killed those that could not escape, which was many hundreds of men'. The king remained a further week in the city and built a second castle on the old Balie site on the other side of the River Ouse. He then returned south for Easter at Winchester, but the leaders of the rebels were still at large.

William's internal problems were compounded by the arrival of a Danish force which struck first at Dover and Sandwich and then moved north along the coast attacking Ipswich and Norwich until it reached the Humber and, in the process, effectively demobilized the Norman fleet. On Monday 21 September a combined army of English and Danes attacked York, storming both castles and slaughtering the Norman garrisons. This event set off a series of further disturbances in the South and West. The men of Devon and Cornwall attacked Exeter, and those of Dorset and Somerset besieged Robert of Mortain's castle at Montacute. These attacks were repelled, but more serious was the attack on Shrewsbury launched by Eadric the Wild and the men of Chester in alliance, once again, with Bleddyn of Gwynedd (**32**). They succeeded in burning down the town, but they were unable to take the castle and moved on to Stafford. In the East a Lincolnshire thegn called Hereward, supported by the Danes, led another uprising centred on the Isle of Ely.

32 Aerial photograph of Shrewsbury showing the Saxon and medieval town within the loop of the River Severn. Roger of Montgomery's castle was built at the neck of the loop, and his abbey outside the town defences immediately to the east of the 'English' bridge.

The Harrying of the North

The situation was precarious for William, with both minor and major acts of rebellion in several parts of the kingdom and a powerful force of Danes still in the East. The monks of Durham fled, carrying with them the body of St Cuthbert and all the portable treasures of their church, seeking refuge in their ancient sanctuary at Lindisfarne. William set about the task of crushing the English Revolt, and in the winter of 1069 again marched to York. He responded using the normal Norman strategy, that is the total destruction of the countryside, creating conditions of starvation and famine. Such brutal methods are particularly associated with William the Conqueror and the Harrying of the North, but had commonly been employed on the Continent from the time of Charlemagne onwards. The strategy of 'harrying' involved the taking of hostages and mass deportation, burning and looting and the transference of the vacated lands to the king's supporters; it was the medieval equivalent of 'ethnic cleansing'. William fetched his insignia and plate from Winchester and spent Christmas 1069 at York wearing his crown in the ceremony customary at great feasts in a demonstration of Norman power. In the North, there was to be little doubt about who was king of all England.

Towards the end of January 1070 the king set out to quell the Mercians. In the snows of February he led his army across the Pennines in a fearful journey which provoked near mutiny among his non-Norman troops. The speed of William's movement once again took his enemies by surprise and he was able to take Chester and Stafford without opposition and built castles there. In the process he devastated the shires of Mercia with the same inhumanity he had shown in Yorkshire and Durham. Even those chroniclers normally favourably disposed towards William were dismayed by his inhumanity; Orderic Vitalis wrote,

on many occasions I have been free to extol William according to his merits, but I dare not commend him for an act which levelled both the bad and the good in one common ruin by a consuming famine ... I am more disposed to pity the sorrows and sufferings of the wretched people than to undertake the hopeless task of screening one who was guilty of such wholesale massacre by lying flatteries. I assert moreover that such barbarous homicide should not pass unpunished.

Simeon of Durham supplied even more lurid descriptions of the destruction, recalling the putrefying corpses which littered the highways. The massacres led to pestilence, and refugees in the final state of destitution fled as far south as Evesham.

After the battle of Hastings the Harrying of the North is perhaps the best-known event in William I's reign, and this episode received almost universal condemnation at the time and afterwards. Surprisingly, few of the surviving leaders of the revolt were dealt with harshly, and several were allowed to retain some of their estates. The devastation of York and Durham is recorded in the folios of Domesday Book in the form of 'waste'. One contemporary chronicler, Hugh the Chanter, claimed that the city of York 'and the whole district round it was destroyed by the French with the sword, famine and flames', while another account records that so many died that there was nobody left to bury them, that there was no village inhabited between York and Durham and that the land remained uncultivated for nine years (33).

After the revolt of 1069–70 there were no more general risings of the English nobles, but William's successful campaign did not entirely dispose of the Danes. By the end of 1071 the Fenland revolt had been suppressed and the shadowy figure of Hereward the Wake disappeared from history into legend. The most important consequence of the English Revolt was its effect on William's subsequent attitude to the English. From then onwards William took every opportunity to replace the English magnates, lay and ecclesiastical, with Normans and other foreigners

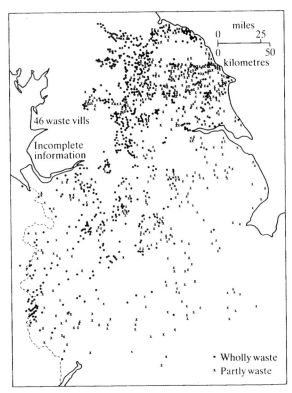

miles
0   25

0   50
kilometres

46 waste vills

Incomplete
information

• Wholly waste
× Partly waste

33 The Domesday record of 'waste' settlements in northern England in 1086. Although some of this devastation may have been brought about by other causes, it is generally thought that the Harrying of the North was mainly responsible. (After Darby)

on whom he felt he could rely. It is the wholesale replacement of Englishmen at the highest levels of society and government and the reflection of that take-over through castle and church building that gives the Norman Conquest its special character.

The end of the revolt also signalled the end of the surviving English nobles: Edgar the Atheling, Earl Edwin, Earl Morcar and Waltheof were all dead by the mid-1070s. Morcar was captured in East Anglia and died in prison, and Edwin was murdered by his own men while travelling to Scotland. Other men of lesser standing continued to serve the Conqueror and a few old English families survived as modest landholders, but for the most part the old English aristocracy met a sorry end. Domesday Book provides abundant evidence that men of substance were reduced to holding, as tenants of Norman lords,

parts of what had once been their own estates. It is this remorseless catalogue of land transference to the Normans, as recorded in Domesday Book, that brings home the magnitude of the revolution. Some went into exile; Abin, the Abbot of St Augustine's, Canterbury went to Scandinavia, and others found themselves as far afield as Constantinople, where by the end of the eleventh century English soldiers had replaced Vikings as the predominant element in the emperor's personal guard and where the expatriate community founded a church dedicated to St Augustine.

During the remainder of William's reign there were two further serious internal threats to the Normans. The first rebellion was in East Anglia in 1075, after which Lanfranc, acting as protector of England, wrote to William: 'Norwich Castle has fallen and its defenders have sworn to leave England within forty days. The mercenaries, who served the traitor Ralph, have begged a similar indulgence. The Castle itself is occupied by Geoffrey of Coutances, William of Warenne, and Robert Malett, with three hundred heavily armed men, slingers and many siege engineers. By God's mercy the clamour of war has entirely ceased on English soil' (**34**). Waltheof, the last English magnate of significance to survive as a prominent figure in national politics, was one of the few to be executed. This was a rare case as, despite his brutality on the ground, William was careful not to create martyrs and was consistently lenient in his treatment of rebel leaders. The second rebellion was in Northumbria, following the assassination of the Bishop of Durham, Walcher, in 1080. William strengthened the defences at Durham and concentrated his hold on the settlement at the mouth of the River Tyne, where he constructed a new castle (Newcastle).

Although internal uprisings did not feature in the final years of William's reign, there was a persistent threat of invasion from Denmark during the 1080s. In response to this, in addition to Newcastle a number of other east-coast castles were constructed, and once more the danger of English support for foreign invasion was

34 (a) South face of Norwich Castle from an early nineteenth-century watercolour. This was painted before the façade of the castle was completely restored, 1836–9. The lower storeys are heavily defended while the upper storeys, which performed a palatial role, were decorated with arcading. (Norfolk Museums Service and Norwich City Council)

(b) The south façade as it is today. Analysis of the building shows that the restoration using Bath stone carefully replicated the original building, which had been in a very poor state of repair. There is considerable similarity between the façade of Norwich and that at Falaise in Normandy, William the Conqueror's birth place.

diminished by the application of the 'scorched earth' policy along the east coast. In 1080 William crossed from Normandy with a larger force of mounted men and foot soldiers than had ever come into the country, according to one source. In the event they were unnecessary as the adversary, the Danish king, Cnut, was murdered in his homeland. In Normandy another threat had presented itself in the form of the French king, Philip, who had taken the area to the east of Normandy. As usual, William responded decisively and sacked the towns of Mantes, Chaumont and Pontoise. The sack of Mantes, however, was to be the last of the Conqueror's military actions. He fell ill in the town and was then taken to Rouen, where the warrior King of England and Duke of Normandy died on Thursday 9 September 1087. It was a year notorious for its fires, pestilence and famine; an appropriate epitaph for one who had brought about such dramatic and at times brutal changes to England through the use of force.

The later Norman kings

William was buried at St Stephen's Abbey in Caen, to which he had given the crown, lance and sceptre of England after the battle of Hastings (35). On his death, Normandy passed to his eldest son, Robert, and England to his second surviving son, William Rufus. William II's succession was a signal for renewed dissent in England, but this time it was in the form of a power struggle based largely around Norman nobles and clerics, who supported Robert. In 1088 Durham Castle was besieged and several royal castles were captured including one of the strongest, Bristol, which fell to Bishop Geoffrey of Coutances and his nephew Robert of Mowbray, Earl of Northumberland. Among other rebels of the time was Odo of Bayeux, who eventually surrendered at Rochester.

William Rufus was involved in campaigns in Normandy in 1090–1, but in 1092 he turned his attention to western Cumberland and Westmorland, which were still under Scottish control. A castle and colony were planted at Carlisle and in 1092 he began to colonize the

area with other Anglo-Norman settlements. William II's reign was characterized by intrigue, dispute and threat of external attack; nevertheless it saw the consolidation of the Norman control of England and military expeditions into Scotland and Wales. As usual both developments were accompanied by the construction of castles and the creation of new towns. William Rufus, like his father, was an expansionist and at the time of his death in August 1100 he was already expressing interest in further overseas ventures, in Aquitaine in particular. One story claims that on the day before he was killed, William was asked where he would spend Christmas that year and he

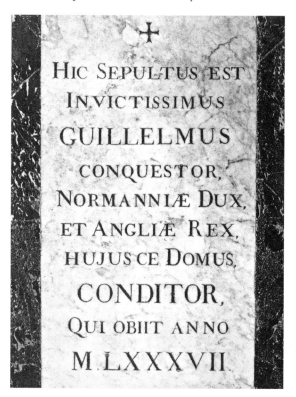

35 William the Conqueror's tombstone in the abbey church of St Stephen in Caen. This monument dates from the nineteenth century – the original tomb was desecrated in the sixteenth century and again during the French Revolution. William's body was brought here from Rouen, where he died on 9 September 1087. His funeral was marked by an unseemly dispute over the ownership of the land on which the abbey was built.

replied 'Poitiers' – an ambition not realized by an English king until later in the twelfth century after the Norman dynasty had been replaced by the Angevin line.

William II was succeeded by the youngest of William the Conqueror's sons, Henry I. Henry was more Anglicized than his two Norman predecessors and married an English noblewoman who conventionally adopted a French name, Matilda. Henry's reign was characterized by the strengthening and formalization of many Norman institutions, in particular the forest laws, which were probably at their most severe during his rule. He was also associated with a number of other legal initiatives and the creation of the network of courts required to execute them (**36**).

During Henry's reign there was no serious internal unrest, but political troubles continued both in England and in France and there followed a further period of military consolidation. After the battle of Tinchbrai (1106) Normandy was again united with England. Construction and refortification were concentrated on coastal defences and along the border with Scotland and Wales; important strategic castles were rebuilt in stone and some defensive town circuits, such as that at Carlisle, were constructed. It was also a period when a

considerable number of Augustinian religious houses were founded in England. A change in the route of main cross-channel traffic occurred soon after Henry's accession, which conventionally had been between Sussex and northern Normandy, to between Purbeck and the Cotentin peninsula. This resulted in the building of major castles at Corfe, Wareham, Portchester and Carisbrooke to guard the new important coastal area, and from then onwards Portchester was the point of all royal departures across the Channel.

The 'Anarchy'

The White Ship disaster of 1120, in which Henry's only legitimate son was drowned, meant that his only legitimate heir was his daughter Matilda, wife of the Count of Anjou (Henry had 21 illegitimate children). Despite the fact that Henry made his barons swear to uphold the succession on his death in 1135 he was succeeded by his nephew, Stephen of Blois.

36 Henry I with his bishops from the contemporary chronicle of John of Worcester. This picture is the third in a series showing Henry's 'nightmare'. In this scene he is depicted in a storm at sea with his bishops; the storm abates only when he vows not to collect Danegeld for seven years. (Corpus Christi College, Cambridge)

Stephen's reign was a turbulent one, but it is probably unwise to think of it as a period of sustained anarchy, as it is conventionally portrayed. Stephen's reputation as ruling a kingdom permanently at war with itself rests largely on the Anglo-Saxon Chronicle's description of Stephen's reign as 'nineteen winters during which Christ and his saints slept'. Despite the troubled political situation new towns continued to be created by Norman lords, and many Cistercian and Augustinian monasteries were founded at this time. Nevertheless, the civil war was hard fought between the supporters of Stephen and his cousin Matilda, and brought great devastation to parts of the country. The eventual settlement was a compromise which meant that Matilda's son, Henry of Anjou (Plantagenet), succeeded to the throne after Stephen's death in 1154. However, the crises of Stephen's reign helped to resolve some of the major problems of feudal settlement of England and paved the way for a permanent legal solution to matters of succession and inheritance, not only at a royal level but throughout feudal society.

On the death of Stephen in 1154 the Norman line in England formally came to an end and was replaced by Henry II, the first of the Plantagenets, who was, however, closely related to his Norman predecessors. Henry had been recognized as Duke of Normandy in 1150 at the age of 17 and Count of Anjou on the death of his father, Geoffrey Plantagenet, in the following year. He married Eleanor of Aquitaine in 1152, thus acquiring control of extensive territories in south-west France. Despite problems with his sons (it was claimed that 'from the devil they came, to the devil they will go'), the Angevin heir to the Norman throne became master of western Europe from Hadrian's Wall to the Pyrenees. Following his accession, Henry played a prominent and at times dominant part in European politics.

Henry's enduring work was in the area of law; royal courts became more efficient and new writs dealing with the assizes helped to stabilize land holding. The power of shire courts and common law became dominant in England. In financial affairs the continuous records of the Exchequer from 1155 testify to the increasingly sophisticated nature of English financial management. Henry did not, however, enjoy much success in his dealings with the Church. The choice of his Chancellor, Thomas Becket, to the archbishopric of Canterbury proved a personal disaster. Becket resisted Henry's reforms, was forced into exile and on his return after a partial reconciliation in late 1170 was martyred in Canterbury Cathedral. Henry was successful in wider political and military activities in Britain. Wales was kept relatively quiet and the Marcher lords, notably Richard Strongbow in Pembroke, loyal. The capture of the King of Scotland during the unsuccessful rebellion by Henry's sons enabled him to assert English overlordship in the northern kingdom. Most significant of all, taking advantage of Strongbow's military successes in Ireland, Henry intervened personally and ultimately established his son, John, as Lord of Ireland.

Historians have placed considerable emphasis upon the premature end of the Norman rule in the mid-twelfth century, but the Norman style of government survived and a complete shift of emphasis in European affairs had been brought about by the Norman Conquest. Richard I (1189–99) visited England only twice as king, once for three months and later for two. Richard's great-grandfather was Henry I and Richard acted in the manner of a Norman monarch, a crusader and a territorial entrepreneur for whom territorial boundaries held little significance. By 1200 the affairs of England and France were interlinked in a manner that would have been unthinkable if the Norman Conquest had not occurred. Conversely, one of the other major lasting contributions of the Conquest was that it had largely severed the cultural and political links between England and Scandinavia that had been so much a feature and a problem of the late Saxon period.

4
Castles and palaces of the Conquest

The King rode into all the remote parts of his kingdom and fortified strategic sites against enemy attack. For the fortifications called castles by the Normans were scarcely known in the English provinces so the English in spite of their courage and love of fighting could put up only a weak resistance to their enemies.

Orderic Vitalis

To the English the Conquest was manifested in the form of castle and palace. These great structures provided irrefutable evidence that society was divided along strictly hierarchical lines, and that the upper layers of that hierarchy were universally occupied by Normans. Hadrian Alcroft in his classic book *Earthwork of England* (1908) summed up the importance of the castle in England: 'next to the Briton the Norman has left the most enduring, the most numerous and the most impressive marks upon our soil'. Castles featured at every stage of Norman England – in the Conquest, in the suppression of Saxon England, and in the administration and maintenance of the Anglo-Norman kingdom.

Private fortifications had developed in France in association with the breakdown of central imperial control, which resulted in local lords waging war against each other. Prominent among these was Fulk Nerra, Count of Anjou (987–1040), who was responsible for building a chain of fortresses in western France, and demonstrating the value of the castle as a means of conquest – an example that was quickly copied by the dukes of Normandy. In contrast the practice of private war and private defence was virtually unknown in England. It is, however, probable that a few of the Normans who accompanied Edward the Confessor to England were responsible for building castles, for example at Richard's Castle and Ewyas Harold (Herefs.). The Anglo-Saxon Chronicle for 1051 records: 'The foreigners have built a castle in Herefordshire in Earl Sweins' territory and inflicted all injuries and insults they possibly could upon the King's men in that region.' This has been interpreted as a reference to a pre-Conquest private fortification at Hereford. Excavations at Richard's Castle failed to provide conclusive evidence of the pre-Conquest origins of the steep-sided motte and bailey there (37), and as no definitive archaeological evidence of pre-Conquest castles has yet been found in England it is safe to assume that castles, as opposed to defended enclosures, were more or less unknown in the England of October 1066.

Duke and castle

In Normandy the dukes and some lords had built private fortifications from the tenth century onwards. References to such fortresses, often known as 'towers', became common in the later tenth century, when some communal fortifications were equipped with a strong point for the local lord. To begin with, the strong

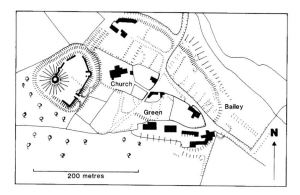

37 Plan of Richard's Castle (Herefs.). The castle on the western side of the plan may have been built by a Norman supporter of Edward the Confessor before the Conquest. The earthworks of the deserted medieval borough, traces of the regular burgage plots and a central market place can be seen within the large town bailey.

point and the lord's residence remained separate, as the lord and his retinue continued to live in a nearby manor house or palace. In due course strong point and residence merged into one and the castle was born. This process has been demonstrated by excavations at Fécamp in Normandy, where in the early eleventh century there was a significant replanning of the defences as Duke Richard II converted what had been a communal fortification into a private castle. At first only the major landowners, counts, bishops and officers of state fortified their homes, but when central authority weakened, the practice spread downwards to the lower members of the feudal nobility.

During the minority of Duke William (1035–47) castle building by private individuals was common and William of Jumièges, one of William's biographers, records that many fortifications were constructed at that time. Once William was of age he set about the destruction of many of the castles that had been built in the previous twelve years and thereafter maintained strong control over castle building in the Duchy. William tried to restrict castle building to his own supporters by issuing licences to build fortifications. Such permits specified that if earth could be thrown on to the

bank from the bottom of a ditch then it did not qualify as a defensive work, but if soil was lifted in stages rather than a single throw, then it became a fortification. The building of high palisades and bastion galleries was forbidden without permission. It was also prohibited to defend rocks or islands, and at critical times William insisted on garrisoning private castles with his own troops. Later Norman kings of England attempted to impose similar restrictions on the building of private castles in an effort to maintain strong central authority.

Horse and castle

The castle was the instrument with which the Conqueror consolidated his grip on England – a task in which he was helped by the use of the horse. The Saxons had used horses for riding and transport, and horses and harness were high-status objects among the nobility. Nevertheless, although King Harold had used horses on his march southwards to meet William at Hastings, when he arrived his men fought on foot. The use of cavalry by the Normans, on the other hand, was critical to their success. The Normans took considerable care to breed and train fighting horses, sometimes in specially designated parks, probably importing thoroughbreds from Moslem Spain. A large number of horses were brought from Normandy to participate in the conquest of England – most importantly a heavier fighting horse known as the 'destrier' was used. A considerable amount of early medieval horse equipment has been found during excavations; notably in Scandinavian graves and in England a large quantity of spurs have been uncovered. Such equipment indicates that Saxon horses were scarcely larger than ponies (**38**).

The horse transformed the castle from a means of passive defence into an instrument for controlling the surrounding countryside. A mounted garrison based on a castle could dominate a large area, and thus castles formed secure bases from which territory could be

controlled. During the Anarchy, John of Worcester recorded that the men of Malmesbury Castle 'exhausted the whole neighbourhood by their ravages'. William of Malmesbury also noted that: 'There were many castles all over England each defending its own district or to be more truthful plundering it.'

Early castles of the Conquest

Most of the castles to be built in England immediately after the Conquest were of earth or timber, either in the form of a motte and bailey or simple earthen ringworks or enclosures (39, 40). The greatest density of earthwork castles was in troubled border areas such as the Welsh Marches, and many were built within a few decades of the Conquest by local lords fearful for their own safety, but also ambitious for the acquisition of new land. Castles were built in a variety of forms reflecting the defensive needs of local lords and the potential of the local topography. Many, perhaps a majority, of the

38 Twelfth-century horseshoes from London. (Museum of London)

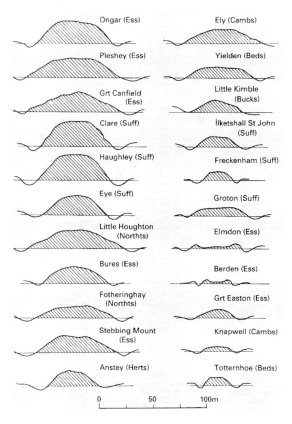

39 Profiles of mottes in eastern England. The diagram illustrates the enormous range of size and shape found in such castle mounds. (After Thompson)

40 Castle Rising, with the palatial twelfth-century keep enclosed within an enormous oval earthwork, which was thought to have been Iron Age until recent excavations showed that it was Norman. (Cambridge University Collection of Air Photographs)

castles of the immediate post-Conquest period enjoyed only a short life-span and were abandoned when no longer needed for protection and their restricted residential quarters were replaced by more comfortable accommodation as soon as expedient.

Some castles were placed in earlier fortifications, in prehistoric hillforts as at Old

Sarum, Roman forts as at Pevensey or Saxon *burhs* as at Wallingford, but most were located on previously unfortified places close to the other symbol of lordly power, the church, and designed to command an estate or a settlement. Some of the earliest fortifications built by William's barons were in the form of large defended enclosures often covering many acres, which provided the space to house a large body of troops. Such enclosure castles were built by Robert of Mortain at Castle Neroche in Somerset (see p. 109), Alan of Brittany at Richmond (Yorks.), Odo of Bayeux at Deddington (Oxon.) and William of Warenne at Castle Acre (Norfolk) (**41**). Such enclosures were intended to keep the household knights together around the baron, but later these castles were normally reinforced with a strong point in the form of a motte or a stone keep. They were then capable of being defended by a

much smaller number of men, as the knights were dispersed to the surrounding countryside, leaving the castle to the immediate household of the lord. An exception to this was Castle Neroche, which was built within a prehistoric hillfort on the western edge of a large royal estate, guarding access to the south-west of England. Although a motte was added to the initial promontory fortress in about 1100, the whole vast castle with its multiple defences was abandoned later in the twelfth century and never reoccupied. Although Neroche was an

41 Castle Acre, Norfolk, headquarters of the Warennes, Earls of Surrey. Immediately above the castle on the photograph are the remnants of a regulated town within a defensive enclosure, and beyond that the ruins of the Cluniac priory of St Mary, founded in the late eleventh century. (Cambridge University Collection of Air Photographs)

important strategic site in the context of the troubled conditions of the half-century following the Conquest, it was not a suitable site for a permanent palace, abbey or town and was therefore left to decay.

The speed of castle building in the immediate post-Conquest period was daunting; by 1086 there were at least fifty recorded castles in England and undoubtedly there were many more which do not appear in the documents. The distribution of these castles partly reflects the first phases of the Conquest and the response to uprisings against Norman control,

42 The giant motte of Thetford Castle (Norfolk). Castle Hill has a mound 25m (82ft) high with attached ramparts 9m (30ft) high and is one of the largest man-made earthworks in England. The castle mound was built entirely of chalk and the prehistoric ramparts were deepened and modified to defend the outer bailey (Ford Street was originally called Bailey End). At the western end of the town the Normans built a ringwork known as Red Castle; thus the town was defended at both ends. The original defences were probably built by Roger Bigod in response to unrest in the Fens led by Hereward the Wake (1069–71). It may have been intended to add a stone keep, but the castle was superseded by those at Norwich and Castle Acre and abandoned in 1174 following the revolt of Henry II's sons and was never reoccupied.

but underlying this pattern there was a clear policy of political centralization not merely in response to specific problems, but also as a means of intimidating the English in an unambiguous statement of Norman superiority. William's initial strategy was to build a castle on the acquisition of each county town. The building of a castle had a profound effect on town and village alike, and the impact of the construction of castles in some towns is recorded in Domesday Book, as many were built at the expense of areas of existing dwellings. One of the seven wards at York was entirely destroyed; at Lincoln, 160 houses were destroyed, and at Shrewsbury 51 houses; all to accommodate the castles or to create a clear line of fire around them. Smaller-scale destruction is recorded at Cambridge, Canterbury, Gloucester, Huntingdon, Stamford, Wallingford and Warwick.

The motte and bailey castle

The most common form of castle in Norman England was the motte and bailey (**42**). The term derives from the Norman French *motte*, meaning 'mound', and 'bailey', the attached 'enclosure'. Despite references to at least forty castles in pre-Conquest Normandy, authentic examples of pre-1066 mottes in France are relatively unusual,

although earth and timber castles are known from places such as Rubercy, Gravenchon, Olivet-à-Grimbosq and Plessis-Grimoult. But the great age of the motte and bailey was after 1066, when many hundreds more were built in Normandy, Brittany and elsewhere in Europe. It is significant that the Bayeux Tapestry, which was almost certainly produced in England in the 1070s, shows five castles in the form of mottes, all surmounted by wooden towers (at Bayeux, Dinan, Dol, Hastings and Rennes). It has been recently argued that a sixth motte is depicted on the tapestry at Beaurain in Ponthieu, where Earl Harold was forcibly taken on his arrival on the Continent in 1064.

The Normans required a form of castle which could be defended by a small number of their troops against a large number of opponents and yet could be constructed with speed, and for these purposes the motte and bailey was ideal. It suited a feudal society where normally it was the estate that was to be defended rather than the settlement. The great advantage of such fortifications was that they could be constructed using materials to hand and if destroyed could be rebuilt quickly. There were no problems in finding quarries or masons or arranging for the transport of stone. All that was required was a team of carpenters and a force of men to dig the defences. The success of the practice of piling earth round the base of a wooden gatehouse or tower located within an earthen enclosure (ringwork) to prevent it being burnt down easily may well be the reason why the motte became one of the principal features of early Norman castles in England. The Bayeux Tapestry shows that fire was an important part of siege warfare and that during William's Breton campaigns the Normans were able to burn down the wooden towers on the top of the mottes they besieged.

Mottes were normally conical in shape, ranging in height from 3m (10ft) to 30m (100ft), and were surrounded by a ditch from which the material making up the mound was normally extracted. There was a wooden bridge leading from the castle enclosure or bailey to the motte;

the latter was normally capped by a tower, which in the early stages was built of timber. The bailey was surrounded by a rampart on top of which a palisade was built and by a ditch or ditches. Inside the bailey there were various structures such as the lord's hall, chapel, stables, a smithy and other ancillary buildings. An early twelfth-century description of the castle at Merchan in Flanders provides a valuable picture of this type of castle and confirms recently excavated archaeological evidence:

> It is the custom of the nobles of that region . . . in order to defend themselves from their enemies to make a hill of earth, as high as they can, and encircle it with a ditch as broad and deep as possible. They surround the upper edge of this hill with a very strong wall of hewn logs, placing towers on the circuit, according to their means. Inside this wall they plant their house (domus), or keep (arcem), which overlooks the whole thing. The entrance of this fortress is only by a bridge, which rises from the counterscarp of the ditch, supported on double or even triple columns, till it reaches the upper edge of the motte (agger).

Work on the motte and bailey site at Hen Domen (Montgomery) over many years has uncovered the archaeological remains of a complicated sequence of timber buildings from the late eleventh century onwards, but is reminiscent of the Merchan description.

There are several regional varieties of motte; in East Anglia, for example, they tend to be tall and steep sided. Typical of this group is the large motte at Thetford, built within an Iron Age hillfort. It has also been shown that a group of timber castles lying to the east of Offa's Dyke in the Vale of Montgomery have distinctive similarities. These castles, which are typified by shallow mottes with small tops, appear to date from the end of the eleventh century. The area, which was under the control of the Corbet family under Earl Roger of Montgomery, was recorded as 'waste' after the Conquest and this

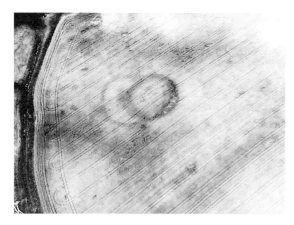

43 The cropmark of a ploughed-out motte and bailey at Hoddenton, Chirbury, close to the Welsh border in Shropshire. Mottes have normally been too substantial to destroy, but some of the early earth and timber castles were levelled for agriculture. (Musson)

homogeneous group of castles could well have been established as a part of a resettlement plan, as the hamlets attached to the castles display clear signs of regulated planning.

The motte and bailey castle remains the most tangible and distinct Norman contribution to the English landscape. Their sheer size has ensured that many mottes have survived in earthwork form as they are not easily demolished. A few motte and bailey castles have been destroyed and can be identified only through the medium of aerial photography (**43**) or excavation, as at Repton (Derby.), for example, where a motte and bailey castle was destroyed to make way for an Augustinian priory. Mottes of all shapes and sizes survive today and are now prized and protected for their historical importance. Their very presence in the landscape has influenced what has superseded them, and the subsequent shape of towns and villages, such as Pleshey (Essex) (**44**) and Devizes (Wilts.) (**45**), has been profoundly influenced by these monuments to Norman confidence and energy.

Stone castles

Yet the most imposing buildings of the Norman era were the great castle keeps. In French such

keeps were known as *donjons* (Latin *dominium*, 'lordship'). It is not entirely clear where the stone keep originated, but it may have evolved from Byzantine and Middle Eastern defensive towers. The earliest reference to a stone castle in France is to Doué-la-Fontaine, built by the Count of Blois about 950. Another early example was built by the Count of Anjou in the form of a two-storey hall tower at Langeais in Touraine about 990. Duke Richard's fortress at Rouen, which has long since disappeared but is depicted on the Bayeux Tapestry, may have provided the model for the great tower keeps of England.

By the middle of the twelfth century many major English castles had either been rebuilt in stone or had stone structures added to them, most notably in the form of a keep, gatehouse and curtain walls. The keep was used for housing stores, armaments and other equipment and providing accommodation on a series of floor levels within a large square or rectangular stone tower. The best known of the great stone keeps is the White Tower of London. The designer of the

44 Aerial view of the motte and bailey at Pleshey (Essex); the village occupies an extended outer bailey. References to burgesses here in the thirteenth century suggest that there was an attempt to create a borough here. (Cambridge University Collection of Air Photographs)

1 Harold swearing an oath of allegiance on holy relics to Duke William of Normandy as depicted on the Bayeux Tapestry. This episode forms part of the underlying Norman theme of the tapestry, that Harold broke his word to William and was therefore not entitled to be crowned King of England.

2 The Winchester Bible, a manuscript which continued the late-Saxon tradition of illustration. (Winchester Cathedral Library)

3 Reconstruction of Norman Westminster, showing Edward the Confessor's Abbey in the foreground, with William II's palace on the banks of the River Thames. At this stage Westminster was quite separate from London, which was still largely contained within its Roman walls. Although Norman kings, like their Saxon predecessors, governed while moving around the country from a peripatetic court rather than from a fixed seat of government, the royal palace at Westminster gradually began to house organs of government such as the Exchequer and law courts. It soon assumed a continuity of use which became permanent by the reign of Henry II in the thirteenth century. (Drawn by Terry Ball. Copyright Dean and Chapter of Westminster)

4 Pevensey Castle (Sussex), the landing place of Duke William's invading army. The castle is now well inland, but the small stream in the foreground probably represents the remnants of a water-course used by the Normans. (English Heritage)

5 The site of the battle of Hastings, with the ruins of Battle Abbey visible on a low rise in the background. It is located on the hill where the Saxon army under Harold made its last stand. (English Heritage)

6 Aerial view of castle and cathedral of Old Sarum (Wilts.), a statement of Norman domination. The large outer bank represents an Iron Age hillfort, which was reinforced by the Normans, who built a castle and bishop's palace in the centre. The base of the original Salisbury cathedral can be seen between the castle and the outer bank (*c.* 1090 and *c.* 1130). The cathedral moved to its present site in the early thirteenth century. (Aerofilms)

7 Rochester Castle keep overlooking the River Medway, with the turrets of the contemporary Norman cathedral in the foreground. The keep, which is the tallest surviving Norman building in England, was built by William of Corbeuil, Archbishop of Canterbury in 1127. (English Heritage)

8 Portchester Castle (Hants). Henry I built the keep *c.* 1120 in the north-eastern corner of a Roman fortress built to guard the 'Saxon Shore'. It was reinforced in the late-Saxon period as a *burh*. In the south-west corner of the enclosure is the church or priory founded for Augustinian canons *c.* 1130. From the twelfth century onwards Portchester became the port for royal voyages across the English Channel. (English Heritage)

9 Norham Castle (Northd.). The Bishop of Durham's superb three-storey castle keep (built *c*. 1160) overlooking the River Tweed which marks the border between England and Scotland. The Tweed provides the northern and western defences to the town, with a deep ravine to the east; a ditch was dug to the south-west. The territory of 'Norhamshire' formed not part of Northumberland, but of the County Palatinate of Durham. The fine castle here was the chief northern stronghold maintained by the bishops of Durham, and like Warkworth started as a motte and bailey, but was later strengthened considerably. (English Heritage)

10 The majestic Norman towers of Durham Cathedral seen from the River Wear. (Woodmansterne)

11 (a) Wolvesey's Old Bishop's Palace at Winchester, started by Henry of Blois (*c.* 1140). The present Bishop's Palace lies to the north-west (top) of the Wolvesey ruins. (English Heritage)
(b) Reconstruction of the Wolvesey Palace, Winchester. In the mid-twelfth century the Bishop of Winchester was more powerful than the king, and his status is reflected in this fortified palace. (Drawn by Terry Ball. Copyright English Heritage)

12 The west front of Castle Acre Priory church (Norfolk).
The blind arcading of four orders is separated by
ornamental string courses. The Cluniac priory was founded
by the Earls of Surrey, the Warenne family, in the late
eleventh century. (English Heritage)

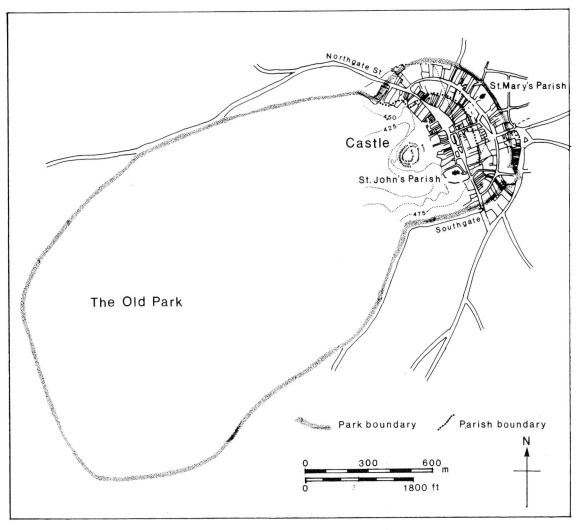

The Old Park

Northgate St.

St. Mary's Parish

Castle

St. John's Parish

Southgate

Park boundary   Parish boundary

N

0   300   600
                              m

0   1800 ft

White Tower, Gundulph, Bishop of Rochester, was also responsible for the other great contemporary castle at Colchester (Essex). The plans for Colchester closely resemble those for the White Tower, where much Roman brick and tile was reused as in London. In the twelfth century large keep castles were constructed at Rochester (1126–39) and Dover (1180–90) (see **25**). Both these great Kentish keeps are notable for the large buildings over the entrance stairs, each of which incorporated a chapel as at Castle Rising (see **40**). Rochester, which has four storeys, is the tallest of the stone keeps in Britain (**colour plate 7**), rising to a height of almost 40m (130ft).

Another remarkable example of a stone keep is at Richmond (Yorks.), where it was built over

45 Plan of Devizes (Wilts.) showing castle, town and park forming an integrated Norman unit, laid out by the Bishop of Salisbury. The original name was *Burgus de Divisis*, indicating that the borough was sited at the divide or boundary between two Saxon manors, Bishop's Canning and Potterne. (Judith Dobie)

an original gateway, which was then blocked, entry being made at the first-floor level from the rampart walk of the surrounding curtain wall (**46**). At Ludlow there was a similar decorated entrance at the base of the stone gatehouse, but this too was eventually blocked and replaced by a causeway and entrance to the east of the tower, which was then converted into a regular keep. Henry I's keep at Portchester is somewhat larger

46 (a) A general view of Richmond Castle (Yorks.), one of the earliest surviving Norman castles in England. (National Monuments Record)

(b) The gatehouse of Richmond Castle, which is incorporated in the original keep. (National Monuments Record/Batsford)

with an elaborate forebuilding to the east and is preserved in part to the top of the battlements on one side (**colour plate 8**). The whole castle, keep and bailey, was built in the north-east corner of the Roman fort there in an arrangement rather similar to that at Pevensey. Many other great Norman rectangular keeps survive, and among the most notable are Bamborough (Yorks.) and Norham (Northd.), Bowes (Yorks.), Canterbury (Kent), Corfe (Dorset), Kenilworth (War.) (**47**), Middleham (Yorks.) and Headingham (Essex).

Castles of the Anarchy

The reign of Stephen was a rare instance of prolonged warfare in England, and it was by and large a war of sieges in which the castle played a central role. The Anarchy was characterized by the 'adulterine' castle or *château adultère*, that is an 'unlawful construction'. The building of unlicensed castles

47 (a) The massive keep of Kenilworth Castle (War.), surrounded by later medieval buildings. Sited at the heart of England, the castle remained strategically important until the seventeenth century. (English Heritage)
(b) The entrance to the keep. (English Heritage)

during the Anarchy presented a major problem to the crown, and in 1154 it is estimated that there were some 274 active castles of which only 49 were in the hands of the king (**48**).

There were extensive siegeworks, and even some churches and monasteries were fortified. It is recorded that monks were ejected from Bridlington, Coventry and Ramsey, while ringworks were erected around churches at places such as Merrington (Durham) and St Martin, Thetford (Norfolk). In 1144 nearly eighty of Stephen's workmen were killed while constructing a fortification of this type against Lincoln Castle. The earthworks which he threw up in front of Corfe Castle in 1139 are appropriately known as 'Stephen's rings'.

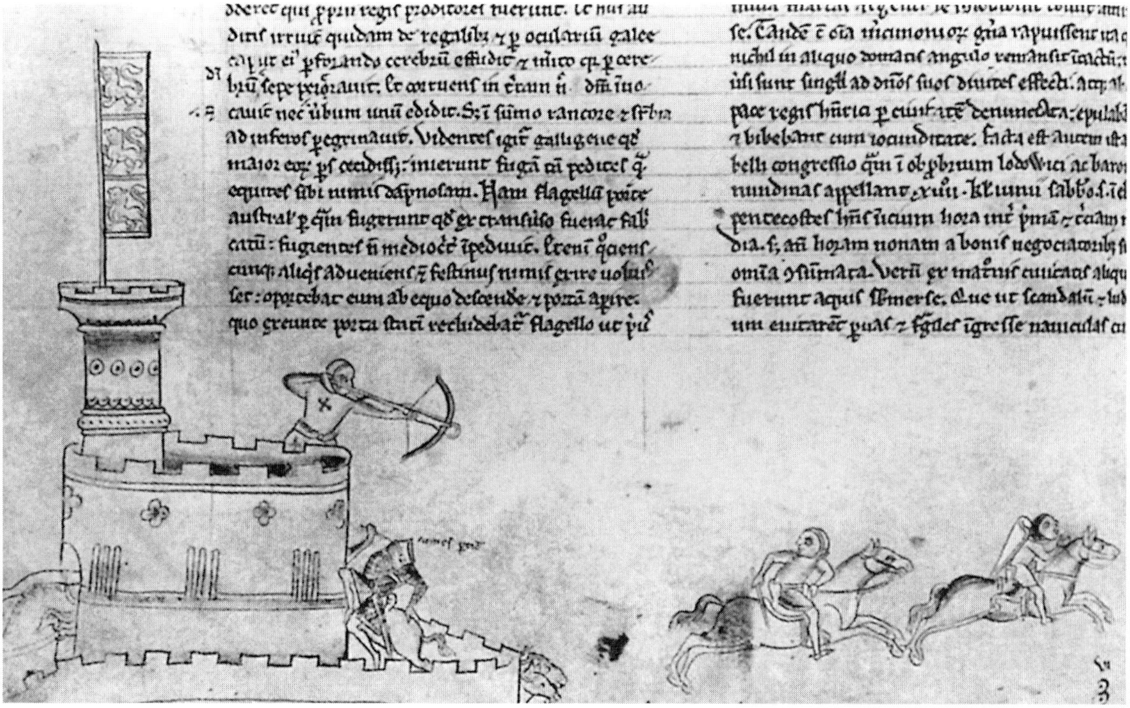

48 A thirteenth-century manuscript showing Lincoln Castle under siege. Lincoln featured prominently in the civil war between Stephen and Matilda. Following his defeat at the battle of Lincoln (1411) King Stephen was captured by Matilda's supporters led by Robert of Gloucester. (Corpus Christi College, Cambridge)

In the first year of his reign Stephen faced sporadic revolts, Hugh Bigod seized Norwich Castle, and Baldwin of Redvers took Rougemont Castle in Exeter, where 'he raised up a very high mount, with unassailable walls and Caesarian towers of hewn limestone'. Eventually both were taken by Stephen, but Exeter succumbed only after a long siege in the course of which he constructed machines for the assault, as well as building a siege ringwork which was clearly recognizable until early in the nineteenth century, but has since been destroyed. Bampton Castle (Devon) held out against the king, who was forced to dig in 'round the castle, post archers to act as pickets by night and detail others to lie in wait during the daytime'. The following years were marked by local uncoordinated risings in which castle after castle was attacked and defended. They included large and powerful castles like Wallingford and Corfe and castles of only local significance such as Harptree, Cirencester and South Cerney.

During the civil war, Matilda's support came largely from the West Country while Stephen's strength lay in London and the South-East, but there was no clear-cut boundary as each area contained castles loyal to the other side (**49**). Wallingford in the South-East remained loyal to Matilda and Barnstaple in the West was for Stephen, but everywhere local feuds and enmities were subsumed within the general conflict. Much of the fighting was in the belt of territory which reached from the West Country through Oxfordshire to Bedfordshire, Cambridgeshire and Essex. This was an area that suffered severely, and it is here that the greatest density of small mottes and protective ringworks can be found. In this region there are a number of castles which were left unfinished, as if their construction had been left interrupted or the need for them had passed before they were completed. For example, Burwell Castle

(Cambs.) was built by Stephen in an attempt to contain Earl Geoffrey of Mandeville, who had seized the Isle of Ely. It was constructed partly on top of an existing village, and traces of two crofts and houses which were destroyed to make way for it can be seen in earthwork form to the north of the castle. In August 1144 Geoffrey 'came with his army to attack a certain castle which had been newly built at Burwell', but was injured by an arrow fired by one of the garrison and died a few days later. The siege was lifted and the castle abandoned (**50**). The aftermath of the wars of Stephen's reign saw the destruction or demobilization of many castles and a significant tightening of royal control under Henry II. Both Henry and his youngest son, John, not only reduced the number of baronial

castles, but almost doubled the number of royal ones. By 1214 it is estimated that there were 92 royal and 179 baronial castles; this change in the balance in favour of the crown was achieved partly by confiscation and destruction but also by construction on a large scale.

Castles in the late twelfth century

The crusades by western Europeans against the Moslems in the eastern Mediterranean resulted in the development of new forms of siege warfare characterized by changes to castle

49 A manuscript drawing showing the wedding of Matilda and the Holy Roman Emperor Henry V, which took place at Worms in 1114. Matilda was only 11 years old at the time. (Corpus Christi College, Cambridge)

50 Aerial photograph of the earthworks of Burwell Castle (Cambs.) which shows the unfinished castle, whose building was interrupted during the Anarchy. (Cambridge University Collection of Air Photographs)

design, and by the middle of the twelfth century new castle forms were being built, incorporating ideas of fortification brought in from the East. This is best exemplified by Château Gaillard on the Seine on the eastern boundary of Normandy, where a castle which incorporated many new defensive features was erected by Richard I late in the twelfth century (**51**). The most notable feature of such castles was the abandonment of the rectangular keep in favour of round towers built as protection against siege warfare. Polygonal and circular keeps as well as shell keeps on the tops of mottes began to feature in many of these later castles. One such example is Conisbrough Castle (Yorks.), whose

original motte was replaced by a fine ashlar-faced keep *c.* 1180 (**52**). However, the cylindrical form of keep, with its variations, never became particularly popular in England, although there are royal examples at Orford (**53**), built by Henry II (1165–7), and Chilham Castle, Kent (1170–4). The closest parallel to the Conisbrough keep is found at Mortemer, near Dieppe in France, a castle also held by the Warenne family, where a smaller version of the Conisbrough keep sits on top of the motte.

Although castle building and repair continued throughout the Middle Ages, the great age of castle building in England was over by 1216 and many earth and timber castles had already been abandoned by this date. The idea of combining the main accommodation in one defensible structure, be it keep or motte and bailey, served the Normans well, but often created extremely uncomfortable living conditions. Consequently,

51 Château Gaillard, Normandy, built at the end of the twelfth century, represented a major departure in castle design with the importation of features from crusader castles in the Middle East. Its fall to French forces in 1204 marked the end both of the English kings' rule in Normandy and of Normandy as an independent duchy.

52 Conisbrough Castle (Yorks.) occupies a scarped natural hill to the south of the River Dearne. The most notable feature is the cylindrical keep built by Hamelin Plantagenet (1163–1201). (Cambridge University Collection of Air Photographs)

53 Orford Castle (Suffolk), a well-preserved polygonal keep designed to prevent undermining. It was built by Alnoth (1165–7) to suppress the rebellious Bigod family at nearby Framlingham and Bungay Castles. (National Monuments Record)

many smaller castles were left to decay as soon as the political climate allowed. The majority of the royal and baronial castles survived, but their functions changed as their military roles declined. Although some castles like Windsor and Kenilworth had their accommodation updated regularly and remained royal or baronial residences, many declined in status to become prisons and arsenals, and eventually quarries as their stone was taken to be used elsewhere.

Palaces

Before the Conquest the English kings owned palaces in towns such as Winchester, Westminster and Gloucester. They also held rural palaces, for instance at Woodstock, Calne and Bosham. The design of these structures was essentially that of the early Saxon hall, as

excavated at Yeavering (Northd.). After the Conquest Norman castles were fortified residences which, in addition to acting as military strongholds, provided living accommodation for lords and their families. The higher the status of the occupant, the more likely it was that the castle would be required to perform other functions such as providing an administrative and judicial centre, and many royal castles were required to house the king's court as well. The difference between a palace and a castle is often difficult to discern. The Tower of London is perhaps the best example: it served the dual function of providing an awesome military base and palatial accommodation for the king and his family. The suite included a hall, chamber, garderobes and chapel. A similar architectural distinction can be seen at Norwich, which also served as a castle-palace. Not all royal palaces, however, were fortified in this way, and the palace at Westminster, which lay adjacent to the abbey, was virtually undefended apart from a perimeter wall. There were also a number of unfortified royal palaces outside London at Woodstock, Kingsholm, Clarendon and Cheddar. Such palaces were often located close to Royal Forests, and served as bases for the royal court and council, which was constantly on the move.

In the eleventh century there were great ceremonial occasions centred on the major palaces, the most important of which was 'crown wearing' in the old Carolingian style. The Anglo-Saxon Chronicle records that William the Conqueror 'kept great state. He wore his royal crown three times a year as often as he was in England: at Easter at Winchester, at Whitsuntide at Westminster, at Christmas at Gloucester. On these occasions all the great men of England were assembled about him: archbishops, bishops, abbots, earls, thegns and knights.' In 1069–70 William extended the Saxon palace at Winchester to perhaps twice its former size, and later in the century William Rufus built Westminster Palace on an exceptional scale. It has been suggested that the balcony on the west front of Winchester Cathedral, although

fourteenth century in date, is the successor of an
earlier Norman balcony, where king and queen
would have appeared wearing crowns. There are
clear indications, however, that such ceremonies
were in decline by the mid-twelfth century, and
this is reflected by the gradual abandonment of
the palaces at Kingsholm and Old Windsor and
even the great royal palace at Winchester.

During the twelfth century it was not so
much the crown but the Church through its
prelates that was responsible for building
palaces. Many of these bishop's palaces were
virtually indistinguishable from castles in the
scale of their fortification. William Giffard,
Bishop of Winchester in the early twelfth

54 The prince-bishop Henry of Blois, King Stephen's
brother, was appointed Bishop of Winchester by Henry I in
1126. In many respects he and several of his fellow
prelates were more powerful than the king. (British Library)

century, provides a prime example of a man
who combined palace building with cathedral
building in his diocesan capital. Giffard re-
established the great complex at Wolvesey, the
former island site which has been the principal
residence of the Bishops of Winchester for a
thousand years. Giffard's work at Wolvesey was
taken over by his successor, Henry of Blois,
grandson of William I and brother of King
Stephen (**54**). In the east range there was a great

hall with a gallery, 'a true hall, a place of gathering, not merely for feeding and sleeping large numbers of retainers, but for meeting and ceremonial. It measured 28m by 9m (88ft by 29ft)' (Biddle). Giffard also created a major palace at Southwark, and the idea of establishing a London residence was subsequently emulated by every other bishop in the land and by many nobles as well. The Bishops of Winchester were responsible for building palaces elsewhere within their diocese; for instance, recent excavations at Witney, Oxfordshire, have shown that the original buildings there date from Giffard's time. Henry of Blois built the castle-palace at Taunton (Som.), which formed the centrepiece of an impressive seigneurial complex including a new town and a priory.

In the neighbouring diocese of Old Sarum (Salisbury) there was a bishop's palace inside a castle, both placed within a prehistoric hillfort, which now provides us with one of the most dramatic monuments in England (**colour plate 6**). The raised circular mound, which formed the inner bailey of the Norman castle, sits in the centre of a huge rampart surrounded by a deep and wide ditch. The exceptional siting of the castle in relation to the outer defences was determined by the geography of the hill upon which it is placed. It occupied the highest ground within the area of the circular fort and could not easily be made to conform to the standard plan of a Norman castle. Roger of Caen built a complex here which included two halls, one for his palace and one for the castle, which he also occupied as well as extensive ranges of other buildings. The hall within the castle was a simple structure without the buttery, pantry and kitchen accommodation which would be expected in a hall designed for entertainment. Roger used stone from his home region of Caen, and the cathedral plan was borrowed from Queen Matilda's Holy Trinity at Caen.

These palaces of the Norman prince-bishops were as imposing as any of those of their lay contemporaries. This reflected their central and sometimes decisive role in twelfth-century England, where the strength that William had invested in the Church rebounded to challenge the power of the crown.

5
Town life in Norman England

At the time of the Conquest about 10 per cent of the population of England lived in towns or communities which were performing urban functions. The extent and importance of towns in late Saxon England has probably been underestimated, with a large number of settlements housing craftsmen, industrialists and traders. Nevertheless, the impact of the Normans was more obviously visible in towns than anywhere else. The immediate impact of the Conquest on many towns was probably little short of disastrous. Domesday Book shows that many towns declined in value between 1066 and 1086. Not only were the Normans themselves responsible for much destruction in rebellious towns such as York, but some of the English rebels, such as Hereward in Peterborough, wreaked havoc in a number of urban centres. Yet within a few decades of the Conquest every county town and many other urban centres were furnished with castles, new cathedrals or abbey churches, new parish churches and stone-built vernacular buildings. The topography of many existing centres was transformed and in addition a large number of new towns were created. The Norman kings saw town and castle as basic instruments of government, and towns had successfully been used in Normandy as a means of centralizing political and economic control; a strategy which was successfully repeated in England and Wales.

In the 250 years after the Conquest the urban geography of England was mapped out in a pattern which survived virtually unchanged until the Industrial Revolution, with the foundation of up to 500 completely new towns. The impetus to urban development was provided in part by the revival of international trade in luxury commodities such as cloth and wine, which had lapsed after the collapse of the Roman economy in the West, but was already well under way by the time of the Conquest. There were many thriving towns in England, particularly in the eastern part of the country. An aristocracy with refined tastes began to create the necessary lines of trade communication to satisfy them. This luxury trade in its turn stimulated exchange in more modest items, and the king, bishops, abbots and secular lords were all involved in the promotion of town life. They sought to foster trade, crafts and industry, and to benefit from the tolls, taxes and rents that resulted from successful urban activity.

The creation of new towns was not always without cost, and several late Saxon towns were casualties. One of the most notable of these was Thetford (Norfolk), whose massive hinterland of central and northern East Anglia was taken over by King's Lynn, Bury St Edmunds and an enlarged Norwich. King's Lynn (originally Bishop's Lynn) was an almost entirely new foundation. In 1086 it consisted of nine salt pans and twelve householders, yet such was its success as a greatly expanded Norman port trading with the Baltic that by the thirteenth century it ranked as the eleventh richest English town. King's Lynn filled a gap in the urban geography of East Anglia, providing a coastal outlet in north-western Norfolk to Germany and the Baltic. Before the Conquest urban functions had almost certainly been carried out in a number of large villages, but the concentration of these activities in one coastal port centre proved dramatically successful. The rise of Lynn and the creation of another thriving new town at Bury St Edmunds (55) together with the expansion of Norwich effectively killed off Thetford, and also diminished the importance of Ipswich to the south-east.

After the Conquest some industrial activities moved out of towns, pottery and textile manufacture representing the most obvious departures. Thetford had been heavily dependent on its Saxon pottery industry, but Thetford's main urban area and its associated pottery industry went into decline after the Conquest. Some activity may have shifted north of the river, but in effect Thetford had ceased to be a major town by the middle of the twelfth century despite its two Norman castles and a Cluniac monastery. Evidence of urban pottery production at Stamford (Lincs.) and a few other places continued until the thirteenth century, but for the most part by the twelfth century pottery manufacture had been relocated to the countryside, mirroring the picture at Thetford.

Norman boroughs

Some 112 places were classified as boroughs in 1086, excluding London and Winchester, which were not assessed in the Domesday survey. But the Domesday survey is selective in its record of towns, and some places such as Bristol, Coventry and Beverley (Yorks.) which can be shown to have been performing important urban activities were summarily dealt with. At Eye, in Suffolk, there were twenty-five burgesses who lived in or around the market place, and there were thirty-five houses in or around the market at Worcester. We hear of stalls in the provision market at York, trading ships at Chester and Suffolk, foreign merchants at Canterbury and a guildhall at Dover, in addition to its harbour and shipping. The small town of Battle grew up outside the abbey within a few decades of its foundation. The plan of the town was typical of Norman design, with a broad cigar-shaped market place running to the west of the abbey gateway with burgage plots on either side. A rental of *c.* 1100 shows that its main function was to service the abbey, but although the occupants were largely English people who had moved in from the surrounding countryside, almost half of them had already adopted continental names.

A more developed form of town plan is to be found at places such as Ludlow (56), where a grid pattern of streets was laid out adjacent to the castle. However, even here there is a suggestion that the original Norman plan was in the form of a broad market place leading eastwards from the castle gate, and that the extended grid plan was added later. Crown involvement in the creation of new towns was at its height in the period up to 1100; subsequently the king played a much smaller role in founding new boroughs. Initially one in three planned towns was a royal foundation, with some 80 per cent of the new boroughs created in the immediate vicinity of royal castles. Some of the early foundations such as Windsor, Arundel and Launceston were completely dominated by castles. At Windsor the royal Saxon settlement at Old Windsor was abandoned and a new castle built on a chalk promontory, which forms the only strong point in the Thames valley between London and Wallingford. Later, the

55 Plan of Bury St Edmunds showing the relationship between the Saxon abbey and *burh* (in the centre) and the Norman town, which was laid out immediately after the Conquest. Abbot Baldwin was responsible for planning the new town, which was made up of a grid lying parallel to the west front of the abbey precinct. Domesday Book records that the new town was in the process of being laid out beside the monastery: altogether there were 342 houses in the demesne of the land of St Edmund, which was under the plough in the time of King Edward.

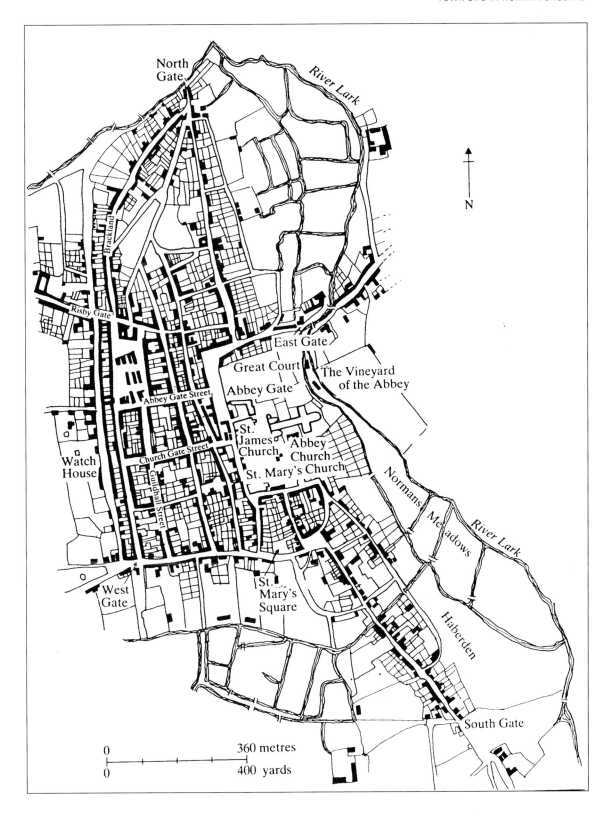

North Gate

River Lark

N

Brackland

Risby Gate

East Gate

Great Court

The Vineyard
of the Abbey

Abbey Gate

Abbey Gate Street

St.
James
Church

Abbey
Church

Watch
House

Church Gate Street

St. Mary's Church

Guildhall Street

Normans

Meadows

River Lark

West
Gate

St.
Mary's
Square

Haberden

South Gate

| 0 | | | | 360 metres |
| 0 | | | | 400 yards |

56 A vertical view of Ludlow Castle and the planned Norman town. Ludlow was a completely new post-Conquest creation which was successfully transformed from a strategic frontier settlement to a flourishing commercial centre by the late twelfth century. (National Monuments Record)

town of New Windsor was grafted on to the newly built castle. Other examples of towns where the castle has had a strong influence on the town plan include Richmond (Yorks.), Launceston (Corn.), Wisbech (Cambs.), Tutbury (Staffs.) and Eye (Suffolk), which have semi-circular street plans, dictated by the shape of the respective castle defences. Huntingdon and

57 Aerial view of Kilpeck (Herefs.) showing earthworks of a medieval settlement which lay adjacent to the castle and fine Norman church (to the right of the road). It is possible that this represents a failed medieval borough, several of which are to be found in the Welsh Marches.

Kilpeck (Herefs.) (**57**) and Caus (Salop) have extensive town defences and earthworks marking the boundaries of former property boundaries. Town walls received relatively little attention in the early phases of the Conquest, the emphasis being placed on private castle fortification. Existing town walls had little spent on them although existing circuits were maintained and only a few new town-wall circuits were erected. Even in the twelfth century there is some evidence that ancient defences were being neglected. However, some towns such as Carlisle, Chester, Canterbury, Hereford and Rochester did receive some allowance for murage costs, but it was only Southampton (close to the royal port of Portchester) which received grants large enough to indicate that large-scale work on the town's defences was being undertaken. It was not until the thirteenth century when there were renewed external

threats from France and Wales that widespread attention was once more given to the construction and repair of town defences; for example the Saxon defences of Ipswich were replaced only in 1203.

Castle and church

Characteristic of Norman castle boroughs is a plan in which the castle sits at one end and the church at the other, normally separated by a large market area. Warkworth provides an admirable example of this design. The first castle at Warkworth was built by Henry, Earl of Northumberland in the middle of the twelfth century at the neck of a loop in the River Coquet, close to its estuary. The present church of St Laurence was rebuilt at about the same time at the northern end of the town, and much of its Norman work survives today. The 100m (330ft) between castle and church is occupied by a broad market area with burgesses' housing on either side. The river forms a natural defence around the settlement (**58**). At Totnes (Devon) the castle dominates the town plan and the outline of the bailey is etched in the street pattern, with the remainder of the old town lying within an extended outer bailey overlooking the bridge across the river (**59**). More modest assemblages of castle, market and church are to be found in the Welsh Marches at places such as Weobley (Herefs.) and Bishop's Castle (Salop). In these circumstances it is not clear if the church was always intended to play a complementary strategic role to the castle, but the sturdy Norman tower of St John Baptist, Bishop's Castle, gives every indication of having the capacity of acting as a fortress.

Normans, Franks and Jews

Although there was not a major influx of Normans or Franks into England after the Conquest, several colonies of French traders were established alongside English settlements. Some of these were founded in existing urban settlements such as Stamford, Nottingham and Hereford. Groups of Frenchmen or French

58 Warkworth (Northd.) occupies a loop of the River Coquet. The castle was originally built by the Earl of Northumberland, and the remains of the Norman great hall lie at the south end, while the Norman church of St Laurence lies at the north end. Between them lies a partially infilled triangular market place and a road along which the traces of regular medieval burgage plots can be clearly identified. (Cambridge University Collection of Air Photographs)

burgesses were also recorded at Dunwich, Hereford, Shrewsbury, Southampton, Stanstead Abbotts, Wallingford, York, Pontefract, Ludlow, Richmond and Northampton. At Hereford, French settlers were introduced by William Fitz Osbern, who granted them the free customs of Breteuil-sur-Iton (Eure), while the old English community there maintained their ancient burghal customs. Subsequently, the Breteuil customs were widely adopted by new boroughs

in western England and Wales in the Middle Ages. Initially there seems to have been a physical separation of the two communities and their markets. Gradually, however, English and French customs were welded together, as were the communities.

At Nottingham, William the Conqueror established 'the French Borough' to the west of the English borough with its own castle, streets and church. Within the new circuit of defences, which encompassed about 120 acres, the northern and western walls of the Saxon fortification were abandoned, and by 1086 the ditch had been built over. But the distinction between the two areas survived throughout the

59 Totnes (Devon). The castle dominates the ancient town, which lies in two semi-circular baileys which run eastwards towards the river. Unusually two original Norman gateways survive in the town. (Aerofilms)

Middle Ages, each borough having its own sheriff and bailiff. The inheritance practices operating in each part were also quite independent, that in the English *burh* still being the traditional 'Borough English' rather than the more usual primogeniture. Nottingham was of particular importance to the crown not least because of its close proximity to the Royal Forest of Sherwood, where William was intent upon establishing a dominant Norman presence (**60**).

The arrival of Jews in England is normally associated with the Norman invasion, and it is believed that they came as an offshoot of the large Jewish community at Rouen. Although Jews probably never formed more than 2 per cent of the population of places such as London and Norwich, they constituted a distinctive, more prosperous element in urban society. During the twelfth century sophisticated credit arrangements were being made to facilitate trade and those Jews would have become extremely rich, a distinction physically expressed in the quality of their housing. Relations with the other townspeople were sometimes strained, and in 1190–1 there were riots and expulsions from towns (**61**). In 1215 London's city walls were repaired with stone taken from the homes of Jews which had been demolished for the purpose. There were Jewish

60 Plan of Nottingham showing the relationship of the Norman borough to the Anglian *burh*. A series of roughly parallel roads run north-east from the castle, a town design subsequently refined and used at New Salisbury.

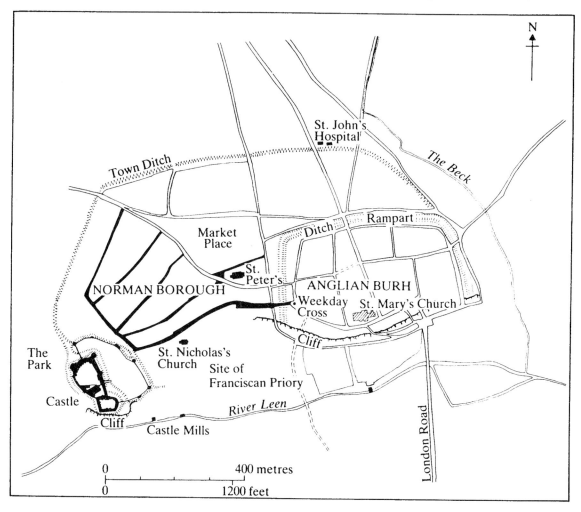

communities within many English towns, but it is as difficult to recognize their presence from archaeological evidence as to recognize the 'Frenchmen' recorded in Domesday Book as separate elements in the towns in which they settled. Cultural divisions can occasionally be identified as at York, where a Jewish cemetery was identified from its north–south burials, and where occasionally specialized Jewish objects have come to light.

Vernacular building

Like village houses, almost all non-military and religious buildings in towns were built of timber, the remains of which have been located by excavation. The sunken cellared timber building, so much a feature of late Saxon towns, appears to have died out after the Conquest and been replaced by regular sill-based wooden buildings. These footings were mainly of timber, but increasingly stone foundations were used. Stone houses were virtually unknown before the Conquest, but they appear in significant numbers in the twelfth century. Merchants needed storehouses, and it is possible to see evidence of their investment in the form of partly or wholly below-ground stone cellars in towns like Oxford and London.

In Norwich, the undercrofts of two fine examples of Norman buildings survive. One of these is preserved beneath the Magistrates' Court just to the north of the cathedral close and was uncovered during an archaeological

61 Early thirteenth-century 'cartoon' depicting Jews and the devil in Norwich. (Public Record Office)

excavation in 1981 (**62**). The other building, known as the Music House, lies close to the River Wensum on King's Street, where its vaulted undercroft is still visible. References to about thirteen other stone houses in Norwich have been found in medieval documents. Most, if not all, of these were probably Norman and may also have been built by Jewish merchants. Perhaps the best group of Norman vernacular town houses to survive comes from another eastern county town, Lincoln, where two fine Norman houses survive in the street which dips steeply southwards from the cathedral (**63**). These too are associated with Jewish activity. A third Norman vernacular building, known as the Guild Hall, lies a mile or so to the south at the end of the High Street. There were undoubtedly many more stone-built houses in Norman towns than have been identified, and recent research has resulted in the identification of about thirty stone houses in Canterbury, and perhaps a similar number in Ipswich. It can be inferred that the richest merchants saw themselves as on an equal footing socially with the rural gentry even though they were not fully integrated into a social system that stressed military service; and that they were possibly even creating their equivalent to a knights' *caput* in the places which they regarded as their particular territory, the towns.

62 The undercroft of a Norman stone house excavated in
Norwich in 1981. It lies on the south side of the River
Wensum and is preserved beneath the Magistrates' Court.
It probably belonged to the Cathedral Priory. References to
over a dozen Norman stone houses have been found in
documents relating to Norwich, and many of these were
probably by Jewish merchants, who were members of
one of England's most important Jewish communities.
(Norfolk Museums Service)

63 The Jew's House, Lincoln. One of three major
important surviving twelfth-century vernacular buildings in
the city.

London

Although Winchester was the capital of the old
English kingdom and still housed the royal
treasury, by 1066, London had emerged as by
far the most important urban centre.
Consequently the Normans imposed themselves
on London, as was appropriate to their new
capital. London received three castles, a new
cathedral, several large monastic houses and
numerous hospitals, priories, nunneries and
parish churches in the century and a half after
the Conquest (**64**). Outside the city, at
Westminster, William Rufus built a great stone
hall for his seasonal palace next to the Abbey
Church of St Peter.

Following a major conflagration in 1077,
Gundulph, Bishop of Rochester, arrived to
supervise the building of the White Tower (**65**).
The new key fortress, whose design was based
on the castle palaces of the Norman dukes of
the tenth century, was of a size not seen before
in England, and it dominated the river and the
city. At the western end of the city, matching the
position and effect of the Tower at the eastern

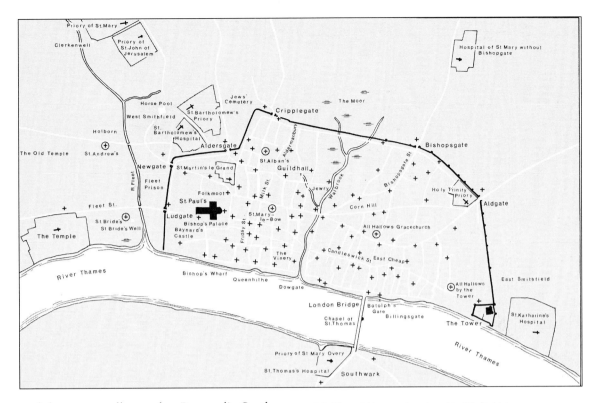

end, lay two smaller castles, Baynard's Castle and Mont Fitchet's Tower. Both lay within the area later given over for the building of the Blackfriars Priory and so their precise sites are not known. Apart from the buildings at Westminster, the other great Norman edifice in London was St Paul's, which Bishop Maurice began rebuilding in 1087. A short way down Cheapside there was another remarkable Norman construction, St Mary le Bow, built by the Archbishop of Canterbury, who established this as his administrative centre in the heart of the city. The beautifully restored crypt survives beneath the Wren church. Just outside St Paul's gate, at the west end of Cheapside, lay the third important religious establishment, which today is remembered only by a street name, St Martin le Grand. This was a college of canons under royal patronage, founded or refounded in the reign of Edward the Confessor.

The first monastic establishment to be built in London after the Conquest was the Cluniac abbey at Bermondsey, founded by William Rufus in 1089, and possibly intended for his

64 Plan of Norman London. (Judith Dobie)

burial. Fragments of this priory were recorded in the nineteenth century, and its twelfth-century church was excavated in 1956. The church was 95m (312ft) long, in the same general form as the mother church at Cluny. During the reign of Henry I, Holy Trinity Priory at Aldgate was constructed, the largest of the three Augustinian houses in London. The other two were St Bartholomew, founded in 1123, and St Mary Overie, founded in 1106, which is now Southwark Cathedral. In the twelfth century, numerous other hospitals and churches were constructed as well as vernacular buildings, but because of fires and repeated rebuilding London cannot boast much great surviving Norman architecture, and one has to look hard to identify the immense Norman impact on the capital. The importance of riverside land in towns has been demonstrated in London, where the shoreline was embanked in the eleventh century. These topographical changes in the later eleventh and twelfth

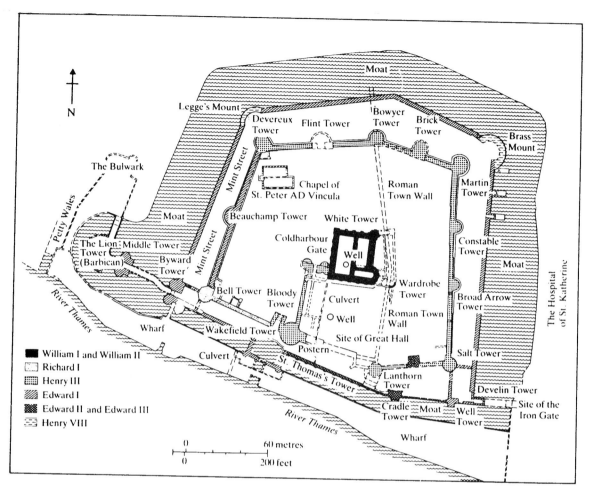

65 Plan of the Tower of London showing phases of construction with the Norman White Tower at the centre. (After Colvin)

66 Detail from the square black Tournai marble Norman font of Winchester Cathedral. The carving depicts an episode in the life of St Nicholas and also has the earliest representation of a ship with a stern rudder, a feature which was significant in allowing the development of bigger ships and new sailing techniques. (National Monuments Record)

centuries seemed to be caused by new works like bridges and castles, and not yet by the demands of new types of sailing vessel with deeper drafts, although recovery of Baltic and Scandinavian wrecks shows that carrying capacities were increasing (**66**).

Winchester

Winchester, the ancient capital of Wessex, was second only to London in importance as a city. Located in the heart of the ancient Saxon

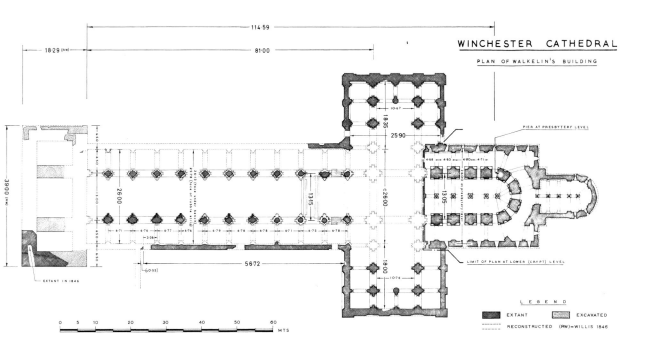

kingdom, it had long performed many of the functions of a national capital, but by 1066, it was already losing some of its powers to London. Nevertheless, to the Norman kings, like York and Canterbury, it remained symbolically important; William established the custom of keeping Easter here. It also formed the base from which rebellion in the west of England was suppressed. Two of the Conqueror's sons, William Rufus and Richard, were killed while hunting in the New Forest and both were buried in Winchester Cathedral. When Rufus died in 1100 it was to Winchester that his successor Henry I came to secure the royal treasury.

The city was transformed in the aftermath of the Conquest. It lay within a rectangular circuit of Roman town walls which had been reinforced in late Saxon times. The building of a Norman castle in the south-west corner of the city resulted in many houses being destroyed. Soon after 1070, the Saxon royal palace in the centre of the city was enlarged to twice its former size, once more involving the destruction of many dwellings and encroaching on the precinct of the New Minster. In 1079, on the other hand, the Saxon cathedral, the old

67 Plan of the Norman cathedral at Winchester. Walkelin, the first Norman bishop, began the cathedral in 1079. In 1093 the relics of St Swithun were transferred to the new building. Earlier cathedrals at Winchester had provided the burial place for many Saxon kings, but William Rufus (died 1100) was the last English monarch to be buried here. In 1107 Bishop Walkelin's central tower collapsed. (Don Johnson)

Minster of St Swithun, which had been completed barely a century before, was demolished and rebuilt on a scale much greater than anything previously seen in England (**67**). Bishop Walkelin, formerly a canon from Rouen, designed an immense building incorporating many elements in keeping with contemporary German architecture. He planned at least six towers, one over the central crossing, one at each corner of the transepts and either a tower at the west end of the nave or two flanking towers as part of an extensive west work. In 1107, just nine years after the cathedral had been completed, the central tower collapsed and much rebuilding was required (**68**).

In addition to its symbolic characteristics, Winchester was also a regular trading,

95

68 The interior of the north transept of Winchester Cathedral showing Bishop Walkelin's severe early Norman work in 1817. At the end of the fourteenth century the cathedral nave was remodelled and Norman pillars were used as the core of the elaborate piers of the new nave. Outwardly the nave retained no vestige of Norman work, but the general proportions and ground plan of the building followed the footprint of the Norman scheme closely. (The British Archaeological Association)

commercial and industrial centre, where evidence of diverted streams through timber-lined channels and pits demonstrates the presence of the cloth industry through the dyeing and fulling processes. Nevertheless, during the twelfth century, the city went into a decline, and royal visits became infrequent. During the Anarchy there was considerable destruction and in 1141 the royal palace was destroyed, removing any possibility of a revival of the city's position as a capital of the realm. Henceforward the principal figure in the

city was to be the bishop. It was Henry of Blois (bishop from 1129 to 1171) who established the bishopric as the major political and economic, as well as religious, power in the city. Henry built the Wolvesey Palace in the south-east corner of Winchester, reusing materials from the ruined royal palace (**colour plate 11**). He was also responsible for building the Hospital of the Holy Cross, in late Romanesque style. Better known as St Cross, it was to become one of the most famous almshouses in England (**69**). Henry also did much to encourage a flowering of artistic work

69 The exterior of the church of St Cross, Winchester. St Cross Hospital was founded by Bishop Henry of Blois in 1136, but much of the present building dates from the late twelfth century and provides not only one of the grandest surviving hospital churches in England but also an excellent example of the Norman transitional architecture as it moved towards the new Gothic. (National Monuments Record)

at Winchester during the twelfth century, a movement which produced fine architecture, metal and enamel work, vestments and superbly illuminated manuscripts including the Winchester Psalter and the Winchester Bible.

Canterbury

Canterbury was the ecclesiastical capital of England, with the metropolitan cathedral and one of the earliest and most important monasteries in the country, St Augustine's Abbey. The Roman defences were standing virtually unaltered at the time of the Conquest, and additionally a great Roman theatre at the centre of the city survived to provide a massive quarry of readily worked stone, and also to dictate the alignment of the medieval street pattern. At the time of the Conquest Canterbury had a population of perhaps six thousand, but as in many towns, arable land was found within the city walls. The city was divided into wards which in the Saxon period had been administrative units of the watch, that is a communal defence system.

The Saxon cathedral was badly damaged by fire in 1067, and soon after his appointment in 1070, Archbishop Lanfranc began to build a new church in the Norman style. In Normandy he had already gained considerable experience as a church builder at Bec; he had also been closely involved in the building of the new abbey church at Caen, which was to form the model for many early Norman churches in England. The new Canterbury Cathedral built between 1070 and 1077 owed much to Caen, and to a great extent that was the responsibility of Gundulph, Prior of St Stephens, whom Lanfranc had brought with him to Canterbury. When the work at Canterbury was completed Gundulph moved to Rochester as bishop and was responsible for building a new cathedral there. He also began work on Rochester Castle and the Tower of London. Subsequently most of the rest of Lanfranc's work was replaced, although elements of it survive; one of his western towers stood until 1834 when that too was demolished

(70). Lanfranc also redesigned the street pattern. The castle and bishop's palace were constructed, and much of the Saxon city swept away. Such was the transformation of Canterbury that within a century of the Conquest, Saxon Canterbury was but a memory.

Norwich

Norwich has been called the most Norman of English towns, and here the impact of the Conquest on Saxon town life is very well illustrated. With a population of in excess of five thousand, Norwich was the fourth largest town in England in 1086. It had grown rapidly as a trade and manufacturing centre during the tenth and eleventh centuries on either side of the River Wensum at its lowest crossing point just above its confluence with the River Yare. Domesday Book records that the town suffered damage by fire and from the disruption caused by the rebellion of Earl Ralph in 1075, and the number of burgesses and freeholders fell by more than half by 1086 from the 1320 recorded in 1066. Some of these had been reduced in status, and by 1086 there were 480 unfree inhabitants of the small-holder class, which was not represented at the earlier date. Additionally, twenty-eight burgesses had fled from the town, of whom twenty-two had moved to Beccles in Suffolk. However, despite these initial setbacks the main impact of the Conquest was to increase Norwich's size, population and importance. Ninety-eight houses as well as associated streets and churches in the south-west part of the Saxon town had been destroyed to make room for the building of the castle. But as the centre of royal administration and power in East Anglia in the long term, the castle at Norwich had a beneficial impact.

Work on the massive stone keep began about 1094 at about the same time that building started on Norwich Cathedral. It seems probable from a comparison of masons' marks that the same workmen were employed on the keep and the cathedral – there are corresponding similarities in the quality of masonry and the use of Caen stone for the

Ćanćebriæ chef defigli
fef den yléfé.

70 Canterbury Castle and the west end of the cathedral as it appears in a manuscript of about 1200. Very little of the original Norman cathedral survives today as it has been built and extended on numerous occasions and only a little exterior Norman work survives today, most notably a water tower built by Prior Wilbert in 1160. (Corpus Christi College, Cambridge)

covering of the walls around a flint core; also, both the keep and the cathedral have wall-passages. However, different sculptors were employed on the two buildings, as the castle carvings are quite distinct from those found in the cathedral. Work was completed on the castle by 1122, when Henry I spent Christmas at Norwich. This great keep was built as a royal palace, and this is reflected in the rich architectural decoration both inside and out. Norwich was by far the most elaborate castle of its time, and it reflected the continuing power and wealth of the Norman kings. The façade at Norwich is similar to that of the twelfth-century castle at Falaise in Normandy, the place where William the Conqueror was born.

The reduction in the inhabited area caused by the building of the castle was offset by the creation of a completely new commercial area laid out to the west of the castle on what had been open fields. In the first instance, this development was intended for those merchants who had arrived in the wake of the Conqueror. These were known as the Franci de Norwic (the Frenchmen of Norwich) and the new area as the New or French Borough, and, by 1086, some 124 Frenchmen were recorded in the city. The centre of this borough was the market place, which remains to this day and which soon eclipsed the old Saxon market area. Three new churches were set up in the French Borough – St Peter Mancroft, founded shortly after 1066 by Earl Ralph, and St Giles and St Stephen, which followed soon after.

Further disruption to the old town was caused by the building of the cathedral when the seat of the bishopric of East Anglia was moved from Thetford to Norwich by Bishop Losinga in 1091 (**71**). The cathedral and its surrounding close covered an area of something like 11ha

71 Norwich Cathedral, a monumental carved figure of a bishop holding a crozier in his left hand and raising his right in blessing. Carved from Barnack stone (Northants), it has traditionally been identified as the figure of Bishop Herbert de Losinga. It is now thought more likely to be of St Felix, East Anglia's first bishop (mid-seventh century), thus emphasizing the long-established line of the bishopric. It was made between 1096 and 1119 and was intended for a niche in the north wall of the transept. (Richard Rowley)

(36 acres), and this was to have a significant impact on the layout of the pre-Conquest town and its river port. Two churches were demolished and major routeways to the North and East were diverted. Despite the initial dislocation caused by the imposition of the cathedral, in the longer term it ensured the pre-eminence of Norwich as the ecclesiastical centre of East Anglia. Thus within thirty years of the Conquest, the Normans had transformed the plan of Norwich by imposing three standard

elements of Norman control on the city's structure (and on its society) (**72**). The political and military might of the king was represented by the castle; the far-reaching influence of the Church was exhibited by the cathedral; trade and commerce were embodied in the French Borough and market place. Norwich continued to grow throughout the twelfth century, and the rapid spread of the occupied area of the town can be seen through the growth in the number of parish churches. By 1200 there were about fifty churches, perhaps double the number in existence before 1066.

Oxford

Oxford had developed as a shire capital in the late Saxon period, based on an Alfredian *burh*, whose outlines can still be traced in the modern

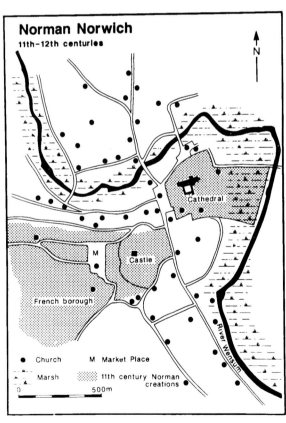

72 Plan of Norman Norwich demonstrating the enormous impact which the coming of the Normans had on the East Anglian town. (The Centre for East Anglian Studies)

street pattern (see **10**). As at so many other provincial towns, the immediate impact of the Conquest on Oxford was negative. The building of a castle by Robert d'Oilly (died 1093) in 1071 led to the complete dislocation of the town's western suburb. Late Saxon houses have been found underneath the castle, implying large-scale destruction of buildings immediately after the Conquest. Additionally the road to the west was diverted around the new castle bailey. The castle itself is situated in the classic Norman setting, half in the town and half outside, with its eastern side incorporating virtually the entire length of the western Saxon defence, while on the west the castle made use of a branch of the River Thames. The castle was thus able to control the town but, at the same time, its garrison had ready access to open countryside in the event of the defences being overrun. The river level was controlled by the castle mill, and the river provided water for the moat which surrounded the castle (**73**).

In the longer term the consequences of the Conquest were beneficial and helped Oxford maintain its importance as an administrative and commercial centre that was the sixth largest town in England. The Normans also improved communications to the town with the building of Magdalen Bridge, which vastly improved trade from London. They had also been responsible for the building of the Grand Pont, a stone bridge and causeway replacing a series of Saxon causeways and timber bridges across the low-lying marshy area to the south of the town which immeasurably improved the approach to Oxford from Winchester, Southampton and the southern ports (**74**).

Under the Normans new churches were built and monasteries founded. By the end of the twelfth century there were some twenty-one churches in the town, and a large number of stone-built houses. There is also archaeological evidence for the opening up of new streets in the twelfth century and the development of extra-mural market areas such as St Giles and Broad Street. Oxford was one of a number of

73 Nineteenth-century print showing St George's Tower, the oldest surviving masonry structure belonging to Oxford Castle. The castle was originally built by Robert D'Oilly and the tower featured in a well-known episode during the Anarchy when Matilda, who was held prisoner here, was reputed to have escaped from the tower over the frozen mill stream and then made her way to join troops loyal to her at Wallingford.

provincial towns where scholars congregated in the twelfth century. The university is first recorded here in 1184, although it was undoubtedly an academic centre before that. There were centres of learning at Exeter, Stamford and Northampton, but the details of their university character are as shadowy as those of early Oxford. It was not until the thirteenth century that the colleges and the structure of the university begin to emerge.

By 1200 the process of town creation and development was well advanced. Undoubtedly the overall level of European trading prosperity would have spilt over into England, even without the Normans. However, it is difficult to

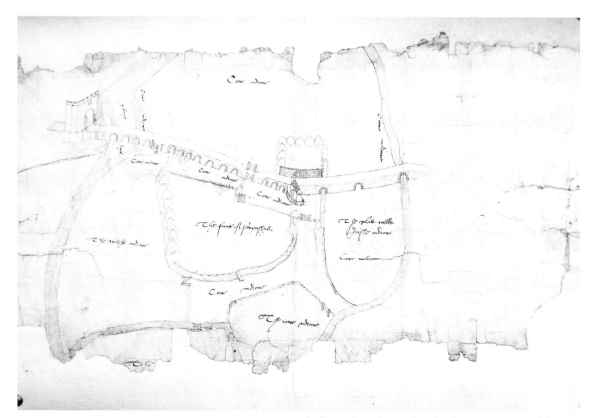

74 A sketch of the Norman causeway in Oxford known as the Grand Pont dating from about 1500. Friar Bacon's tower lies on the left of the plan and the arches of the bridge extend across several tributaries of the River Thames. The Grand Pont was probably the most impressive civil engineering achievement in eleventh-century Europe, but now lies hidden below the Abingdon Road, along whose length it extends for almost a mile. (Brasenose College Library)

believe that the scale of urbanization would have been so great. The Normans found towns flexible enough both to exert control over a region and to exploit it commercially. Thus towns which the Normans originally created to dominate politically, strategically and administratively were soon adapted to become important centres of regional economic growth and control.

6
The Norman Church

It is in these buildings rather than the castles that Norman investment, sense of grandeur, self-confidence and downright arrogance are best seen.

Hinton

The Norman Conquest brought great changes to the English Church, characterized by a building campaign of enormous intensity and vigour. Cathedrals, abbeys and parish churches were destroyed and rebuilt throughout the land on a scale hitherto unknown either in England or indeed in Normandy. Between 1070 and 1100 work on thirty cathedrals and major monastic churches began in England, and many of these were completed by the first decade of the twelfth century. New cathedral churches went up alongside Saxon cathedrals at places such as Winchester, Exeter, Wells and Worcester. The Norman builders were so thorough in their reconstruction that there is virtually no pre-Conquest architecture surviving in any English cathedral or abbey. This was a momentous achievement by any standards. In addition the Conquest provided the opportunity to start afresh with a virtually new architectural style – Norman Romanesque – and produced one of the most important periods in English building history. The radical redistribution of land after 1066 provided ready opportunities for the spread of monasticism. The Conquest turned many local lords into powerful magnates who had significant surplus wealth at their disposal.

Some of this wealth was spent on the endowment of churches, cathedrals and abbeys, and some of the surplus land, frequently of marginal value, was painlessly given to the newly found monasteries in order to secure for the donors a place in heaven.

The Norman take-over of the English Church

William the Conqueror's early dealings with the Church in England were cautious; for example, the Saxon Stigand was retained as Archbishop of Canterbury until 1070, but soon William began appointing French clerics to the highest positions, and after the English Revolt this process accelerated. One by one leading English churchmen were removed. Remigius from Fécamp was made Bishop of Dorchester in 1067, in 1070 Thomas, from Bayeux, became Archbishop of York, and Walkelin, Bishop of Winchester. In the same year the king secured papal support for other major ecclesiastical changes and Archbishop Stigand and five other English bishops were removed. William appointed Lanfranc, Abbot of Caen, to Canterbury. So complete was the foreign take-over of the Church that William of Malmesbury, writing fifty years after the Conquest, claimed that 'England has become a residence of foreigners and the property of aliens. At the present time there is no English earl nor bishop nor abbot; strangers all they prey upon the riches and vitals of England.' By 1086 of the fifteen diocesan bishops, eleven were Norman, two were from Lorraine, one was Italian and only one was English.

The Norman Conquest resulted in radical reform to the Saxon Church which was to render the Conquest as complete intellectually as it was politically. This reorganization resulted in far greater papal involvement than had been the case in the Saxon Church. Lanfranc was the critical figure in the reform of the English Church, just as he had been in reforming the Norman Church before the Conquest. His insistence on control of the whole English Church mirrored William's secular control of the whole of England. He obtained written promises of obedience from each new consecrated bishop and he insisted that York should recognize the superiority of Canterbury. Perhaps the most obvious sign that the English Church was being brought into line with the European Church was in the transfer of cathedral churches, often from remote locations or from small towns to urban centres.

In the Church, as in secular society, Englishmen were usually relegated to lesser roles. Many did survive in monasteries where a small articulate minority was able to maintain the tradition of English historical writing as Latin took over as the language of administration, both secular and ecclesiastical. One of the most influential Englishmen of the twelfth century was Stephen Harding from Sherborne, who become Abbot of Cîteaux. Other Anglo-Normans were to succeed abroad in the Church in the twelfth century: for instance, Walter 'Ophamil' and later his brother Bartholomew became Archbishops of Palermo in Sicily in the late twelfth century, and ironically became involved in a power struggle with the Norman kings there. However, at the local level the vast majority of English parishes continued to be served by English clerics who sometimes found the lack of even the most rudimentary French and Latin a severe handicap.

Romanesque church architecture

The style of architecture which in England is almost universally known as Norman was introduced from the Continent in the middle of the eleventh century, where it was known as Romanesque, or more simply as Roman. Its origins are to be found in the Classical and neo-Classical buildings of northern Italy and Germany, whose influence was transferred to Burgundy in the early eleventh century and then taken on to Normandy by clerics such as William of Volpiano. Romanesque architecture had made its appearance in England prior to the Conquest at Westminster Abbey and possibly Waltham Abbey. Among the Normans Edward brought with him to England on his accession to the throne was Robert of Jumièges, who was made first Bishop of London and then Archbishop of Canterbury. Robert had been involved in the initial stages of the rebuilding of the abbey church of Jumièges on the Seine, and clearly his influence was very important when Edward commissioned a new abbey church at Westminster and 'chose to have for himself a place of burial there'. Both new churches were to be built in the Norman Romanesque style, and in the case of Westminster this represented a major architectural innovation in England (see p. 32).

The massive ruins at Jumièges on the Seine provide a good impression of what the Confessor's abbey would have looked like (see 5). As with many successful Romanesque churches, Edward's church was rebuilt in the Gothic style in the thirteenth century and only fragments of Norman work survive in the monastic buildings, although excavations earlier this century demonstrated the structural similarities with Jumièges (75). There are considerable portions of the Norman monastic offices surviving at Westminster, albeit in a modified form. Although the architecture at Westminster was purely Norman in origin, some of the decorative details, such as the unique use of glazed tiles, suggests that the ornamentation may have been adopted for English tastes and provides an indication of the direction in which Anglo-Norman architecture was to develop subsequently. From 1160 Westminster became the English coronation church and later the

principal royal mausoleum, and the royal palace nearby became the main site of the Exchequer in Henry II's reign.

The Romanesque church depended upon the use of arcades of rounded arches. The main and most impressive arcade was surmounted by a second stage known as the triforium, and that in turn carried the clerestory, where the wall could be pierced with windows. Norman architects were skilful in varying the proportions of these storeys. Blind arcading with pillar and arch constructed against a blank wall was also a very popular form of decoration, examples of which can be seen at Gloucester Cathedral (1089–1100), the chapter house at Worcester Cathedral (pre-1125) and the chapter house at Wenlock Priory (mid-twelfth century) (**76**).

75 (a) Excavations in Westminster Abbey during the 1930s revealed the foundations of the original late Saxon pillars. This work confirmed the close design relationship between Westminster and Jumièges in Normandy. (National Monuments Record)
(b) Plan of Westminster Abbey showing Edward the Confessor's church (in dark black) in relation to the existing abbey church.

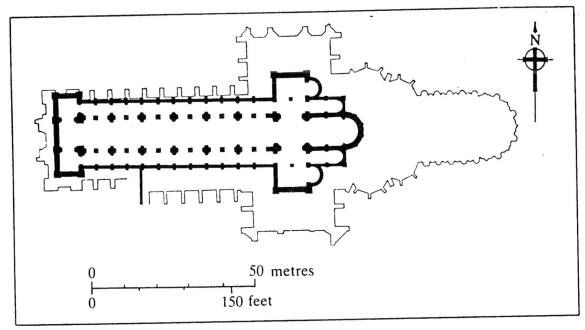

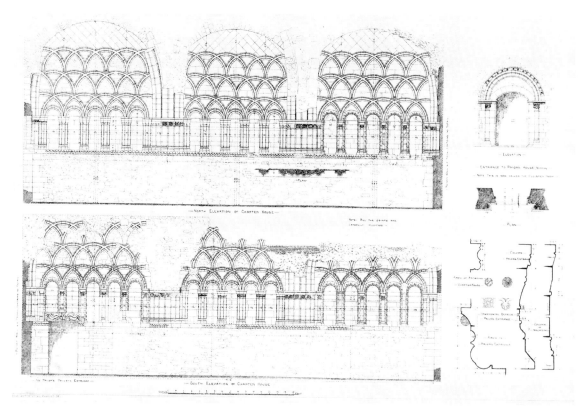

76 (a) Blind arcading in the chapter house at Wenlock Priory (Salop) as it appeared in a drawing for *The Builder* in 1888. (National Monuments Record)

(b) Surviving blind arcading from the exterior of the stairway at Castle Rising (Norfolk). Surviving secular work of this type is relatively unusual, emphasizing the high status of the castle here.

One of the chief advantages of the new Romanesque over previous building styles was the introduction of larger vaulting spans which enabled the construction of wider buildings. Romanesque masons introduced other innovations, including the choir with an ambulatory and radiating chapels enclosing the eastern apse. This was ideal for the display of shrines and relics, and for the easy circulation of large numbers of pilgrims. Anglo-Norman Romanesque architecture made a major contribution to the evolution of rib vaulting, which became an essential feature of later medieval architecture. Romanesque churches needed thick walls in order to carry the weight of stone vaulting, and it was a development of the pointed arch which enabled different methods of support to be developed and eventually for piers and columns to replace the heavy walls.

After it had been introduced to England the Romanesque style did not remain static. In the first instance Norman church architecture is barely discernible from military and vernacular stone architecture (77). It was characterized by the use of rounded arches, massive supports and heavy, solid walling, and for the most part it was plain, lacking in decoration. Such decoration as there was tended to be in the Carolingian or sub-Classical style with little figurative depiction. There is a clear fusion between Norman, Saxon and Viking motifs both in decoration and in structural design during the first half of the twelfth century, and from about 1130 the flamboyant period of English Romanesque decorative carving begins, perhaps initiated by the spread of continental craftsmanship from the Cluniac monastery at Lewes. The zig-zag 'chevron' motif was at the centre of this development and during the twelfth century became increasingly sophisticated and elaborate, and from the later Norman period hundreds of richly carved doorways, chancel arches, corbel tables, arcades and windows survive (78).

Romanesque architecture derived its inspiration from many sources, including book

77 The heavy rounded pillars of the early Norman church belonging to Shrewsbury Abbey, founded by Roger of Montgomery in about 1080. Early church architecture was virtually indistinguishable from that employed in contemporary castles. Roger was also responsible for building Shrewsbury Castle at about the same time, but little of his original architecture survives there.

illumination, goldsmiths' work, ivory carving and wooden sculpture. The fact that craftsmen were trained in several skills is demonstrated in an artist's manual, *De Diversis Artibus* (*c.* 1100), which demonstrates that contemporary artists were proficient in several different fields. Most aspects of Romanesque art and architecture were deeply religious, but also incorporated secular, sometimes crude or humorous images, and a taste for the fantastic and grotesque, often in the form of mythical beasts. Capitals also incorporated a wide range of design from a simple cushion shape to ornate spiral designs or vivid sculptures of biblical scenes and incidents from the cults of many

78 The famous west front of St Mary, Iffley, Oxford. The church was built in the second half of the twelfth century but was heavily restored in the nineteenth century when the rose window was inserted, apparently on the basis of earlier drawings showing surviving traces of an original Norman round window.

often profound, and their architectural influence can be detected in parochial churches over a wide area. Eventually, in the later part of the twelfth century the highly flamboyant Romanesque architecture gave way to the more graceful Gothic style imported from the Isle de France, in England classified as Early English.

The Norman attitude to the Saxon Church

The politics of the Saxon Church posed a problem to the Normans. Pluralism (the holding of two or more positions at the same time) was common. Stigand, Archbishop of Canterbury in

79 The south doorway of St Mary and St David, Kilpeck (Herefds.). The best surviving architecture of the Hereford school of Norman sculpture, whose work is to be found in a number of mid-twelfth-century churches in the Welsh Marches. The exotic range of carving found in the columns, capitals and corbels at Kilpeck echoes the Romanesque architectural style found along the pilgrimage route to Santiago de Compostela in north-western Spain.

saints, but also secular themes such as the signs of the zodiac. It was the inventive and lively character of much twelfth-century church decoration that prompted the austere St Bernard of Clairvaux to complain: 'For God's sake, if men are not ashamed of these follies, why at least do they not shrink from the expense?'

There were marked regional variations in style, and the work of distinctive schools of sculpture can be identified. One of the most studied is the Herefordshire school, whose best surviving work can be seen today at Kilpeck Church (Herefs.) (**79**), but characteristic elements of their designs can be found in a dozen or so other parish churches and priories in different parts of the Welsh Marches and the Midlands. The influence of certain churches, such as Reading Abbey in the Cluniac style, was

1066, held both Canterbury and Winchester Cathedrals and also received revenues from other foundations including Glastonbury, St Albans, St Augustine's at Canterbury and Ely. Both Harold and William I were crowned by Ealdred, the Archbishop of York, rather than risk a challenge to their title to the throne because of Stigand's unsteady claim to the Canterbury see, although some authorities believe that he did participate in William's coronation, but that his role was suppressed later by Norman chroniclers. He is also shown on the Bayeux Tapestry as crowning Harold, which was probably Norman propaganda designed to reinforce the illegality of Harold's claim to the throne.

Apart from the politics and personalities, there was the problem of a conflict of cultures. The English Church was firmly Saxon in its loyalties and spiritualities. The saints who were revered in pre-Conquest England were Saxon or Celtic. The English language was widely used in liturgy and there were strong vernacular traditions in sculpture and manuscript illustration. Nevertheless, English churchmen, especially in the South, were aware of developments in Europe. Despite some strong links between some English and French monasteries the Normans regarded the Church of their newly conquered kingdom as insular and remote. During the Harrying of the North it is reported that William's men treated the metropolitan cathedral at York as 'an object of scorn'. In the first instance, at least, the Normans also had little respect for the Saxon saints. Lanfranc removed the majority of Saxon saints' days from the calendar of Christ Church, Canterbury, and the rededication of churches to saints familiar to the Normans, such as Stephen, Catherine and Michael, was commonplace. At St Albans Abbot Paul broke up the tombs of his Saxon predecessors, whom he referred to as 'uncultured idiots', and the new Norman Abbot of Abingdon tried to obliterate the memory of the Saxon St Aethelwold, whom he called 'an English rustic'.

Some of the early antagonism may have been fuelled by the Church's association with

rebellion at places such as Durham and Ely. But it is also clear that after his coronation in addition to taxing it William robbed the English Church of much portable treasure in order to embellish his victory parades in Normandy. Domesday Book also shows that large areas of monastic estates were confiscated and passed to Norman lords. Such insensitive action naturally led to bitterness and it was reported that at some monasteries, such as Glastonbury and St Augustine's, resentment erupted into violence.

Norman disregard for a sacred site at Montacute (Som.) was alleged to have been the provocation for the rebellion in the South-West. In 1068 Robert of Mortain built a castle on a site where earlier in the eleventh century a reputed fragment of the Holy Cross had been found. The holy relic was sent to Waltham (Essex), where Harold endowed a religious house dedicated to the Holy Cross, and the Holy Rood of Waltham became an object of popular veneration and pilgrimage. 'Holy Cross' was the battle cry of Harold's army both at Stamford Bridge and Hastings, and Harold's body was eventually laid to rest at Waltham. The building of a castle on the spot where the legendary relic had been found was seen as a final insult to the defeated English and produced a fierce local reaction, which was equally fiercely suppressed.

Pilgrimage

After the Conquest many if not most parish churches were rededicated to saints with whom the Normans were familiar. St Michael was a particularly popular dedication. Nevertheless, Norman bishops soon recognized the economic advantages of maintaining Saxon traditions for the prosperity of their cathedrals and churches. Saints' relics provided an attraction to large numbers of pilgrims whose custom to the Church, the town and the villages on the road to the shrine was most welcome. The enormous popularity of the pilgrimage to Santiago de Compostela in north-western Spain demonstrated the benefits which came with the successful exploitation of relics. The cult of St James at Santiago was promoted by the great French monastery at Cluny and attracted tens of thousands of pilgrims from throughout Europe each year. In England pilgrimages were on a more modest scale and the pilgrims were largely from Britain; they were not initially attracted to the European saints introduced by the Normans. Hence the importance of the old Saxon saints. The Saxon cults of St Cuthbert at Durham, St Etheldreda at Ely and St Swithun at Winchester were soon being cultivated by the Normans, who rehoused their relics in their new building. The cults of two Saxon martyr kings were also popular, St Edmund at Bury St Edmunds, and St Edward, who ruled England from 975 to 978, at the nunnery of Shaftesbury.

Most pilgrimage centres tended to be in towns or in large churches or abbeys, but there were other local examples where folk memory of a Saxon saint was reinforced by Norman piety. One of the most important rural pilgrimages was to the Chapel of Our Lady at Walsingham (Norfolk), a village where miracles associated with the Virgin Mary were reported from before the Conquest. It was unrivalled in England as a centre of pilgrimage, being visited by every monarch from William I to Henry VIII. But pilgrimage centres of a much more modest nature were to be found throughout Norman England.

The Normans did manage to develop a few pilgrimage centres based on non-Saxon saints who were canonized after the Conquest such as the shrine of Bishop Hugh at Lincoln (died 1200), but by far the most successful of these was the cult of Thomas Becket at Canterbury. Murdered in 1170, he was canonized in 1173 and his cult was carefully cultivated immediately afterwards. The pilgrimage to Canterbury became widely popular in the late twelfth century and remained so throughout the later Middle Ages. Cures were recorded meticulously and systematically and the cathedral grew rich from the offerings of the pilgrims. A new east end was required to house Becket's shrine and accommodate the increasingly large number of pilgrims. Churches on recognized

pilgrim routes also prospered as staging posts on the road to Canterbury. Such was the immediate and international attraction of the Becket story that an image of the new saint was painted in the new cathedral at Monreale in Sicily, built by a very different Norman king, William the Good, in about 1185.

Norwich Cathedral, a major centre without holy relics, devised the story of William, a 12-year-old supposedly killed by Jews in 1144. A monk at Norwich, Thomas of Monmouth, described the martyrdom in gruesome detail even though there appears to have been no substance to the story. Thomas recounted a dream in which Bishop Herbert Losinga appeared to him saying that in the past they had to acquire lands for funding the cathedral through rents, but now they had relics. The boy's body was first buried on the south side of the high altar, but it was later moved to one of the radiating chapels on the north-east because access for crowds of pilgrims was easier there. The cult of St William was very popular among local people, especially in the 1150s and 1160s, but never developed on the same scale as cults elsewhere and later dwindled into insignificance.

Cathedrals and abbeys of the Conquest

In late Saxon England there had been a strong sentimental attachment to buildings with a long history of sanctity. Much money was spent on the internal enrichment of Saxon cathedrals and abbeys, but when it was necessary to enlarge them it was usual to extend or build a supplementary building close by rather than start afresh. It is recorded that Bishop Wulfstan of Worcester (1062–95), the only English survivor of the Norman take-over, cried at the prospect of having to destroy his ancient cathedral to make way for a new Norman building. Many Saxon cathedrals were very small and would have been virtually indistinguishable from parochial minster churches, apart from their function of housing the bishop's seat.

Just as the secular authority of the Normans was imposed on England by the building of castles, so their ecclesiastical authority was imposed by the construction of new churches. The leaders of the new Anglo-Norman Church were builders, administrators and men of ambition, and rivalry between the new bishops played no small part in the rebuilding process. Work on new cathedrals was started by the new prelates within half a century of the Conquest at Canterbury (Archbishop Lanfranc, 1070–80) (see p. 98), York (Archbishop Thomas, 1070–1100), Winchester (Bishop Walkelin, 1070–98) (see pp. 95–7), Durham (Bishop William of St Calais, 1086–1107), Rochester (Bishop Gundulph, 1077–1108) (80), Salisbury (Bishop Osmund, 1078–99), London (Bishop Maurice, 1086–1107), Lincoln (Bishop Remigius, 1086–92), Bath (Bishop John, 1090–1127), Norwich, Bishop Losinga (1095–1119) (see pp. 98–100) and Worcester, Bishop Wulfstan (1062–95).

At St Albans (which became a cathedral in 1540), shrine of the first British martyr, work on the Norman church started in the 1070s and 1080s with the erection of an almost military early Norman tower, much of it built in reused Roman material, and the outer walls of the chancel, transepts and naves can still be seen. This is the strong primitive architecture of the Conquest – there is no structural ornament beyond the most simple and a little reused Saxon material. In London in 1087 work began on the cathedral of St Paul's, which, when it was eventually completed in the thirteenth century, was the longest church in Christendom until its destruction during the Great Fire of London (1666). Elsewhere there was a considerable amount of innovation, and some of the most original ideas emerged in the devastated North.

Durham Cathedral, perhaps the masterpiece of Romanesque architecture in western Europe, was started in 1093 to provide a major religious centre for the North beyond York and a suitable shrine for St Cuthbert of Lindisfarne. The rib-vaulted chancel was completed by about 1104, the crossing and north transept by 1110, and the south transept and the celebrated nave, which was started about the same time, by 1133. The

80 The ornately decorated doorway at Rochester Cathedral (Kent) dating from the second half of the twelfth century. (National Monuments Record)

west towers and the Galilee chapel, housing the bones of the Saxon historian Bede, were completed by about 1170. Durham incorporated a number of new important architectural and decorative features including the incised drum piers of the nave (81). Incised piers were an ambitious feature which was copied only in relatively few places, such as at Norwich Cathedral, Selby Abbey (Yorks.), Waltham Cross (Essex) and Lindisfarne or Holy Island (Northd.). Durham Cathedral's importance as part of the Norman achievement is threefold, firstly, through its general location on the edge of the Norman world, secondly, through its local siting dominating a high promontory on a meander of the River Wear, and thirdly, through its totality as a virtually complete Norman building. It was a statement that the Norman writ in the early twelfth century ran from Durham in the North-East to Exeter in the South-West.

81 (a) Interior of Durham Cathedral nave showing the incised drum piers, a design feature developed in England in the early twelfth century, and claimed by many as one of the highest achievements of Norman architecture. (National Monuments Record)
(b) Incised pier from the ruins of the Cluniac priory at Castle Acre (Norfolk).

The cathedral begun at York in about 1080 differed from other known major Anglo-Norman churches of the period in possessing no aisles. As a result the clear span was huge, about 13m (45ft), and the transept incorporated a central crossing with a tower above of an unprecedented area of over 600sq m (2000sq ft). York presented a new concept so far as the dimension of English churches was concerned. Its span rivalled those of the contemporary European churches at Cluny, St Ambrogio,

Milan, and Santiago de Compostela in Spain. These great churches demonstrate one of the major differences between the large Romanesque churches of Normandy and England. In England the churches tended to be very long. Westminster Abbey nave had twelve bays and Winchester thirteen, whereas Jumièges and Caen had only eight. The great Norman cathedrals of England represented a form of imperial architecture, and were closer in size to the great imperial churches of Germany than those of Normandy.

The monastic revolution

The rebuilding of new cathedrals was accompanied by the rebuilding of Saxon abbeys and the foundation of many new institutions. In many cases there was little architectural difference between cathedrals and abbeys as many cathedrals had communities of canons attached to them and therefore required similar facilities and shared a common basic design. Although cathedrals were based in towns and many monasteries, particularly new ones, were located in the countryside, the Conquest marked the start of a new phase of monasticism, with the creation of hundreds of new institutions in the eleventh and twelfth centuries (82). It was mixture of piety and policy that moved the king and the Norman aristocracy to donate part of their newly acquired property to monasteries. The primary motive was that of safeguarding the souls of the benefactor and his family. To found and endow a community of monks was calculated to ensure a perpetual fund of intercession and merit both during life and after death. One of the gravest sins was homicide, even if the killing had taken place in legitimate battle. The papal legate Bishop Ermenfrid in 1070 prescribed penances for those who had fought at Hastings with this proviso: 'Anyone who does not know the number of those he wounded or killed

must, at the discretion of his bishop, do penance for one day in each week for the remainder of his life; or, if he can, let him redeem his sin by perpetual alms, either by building or by endowing a church.' Clearly, this prompted many Norman settlers to donate land to new monasteries at home or to endow new foundations in England.

The first to arrive were the Norman monks from abbeys such as Bec and Jumièges, many of whom were men who combined native energy and organizational ability with a zeal for a new religious movement. Some of them were carefully chosen to go to reinforce existing monasteries and their daughter houses, while others came to colonize new foundations. It has been estimated that between 1066 and 1130 about forty abbots and priors of cathedral

82 Chapterhouse doorway at Furness Abbey (Lancs.). The rather heavy chevron or zig-zag design is typical of twelfth-century Norman architectural work. (English Heritage)

monasteries were recruited directly from twenty-six Norman abbeys, and that fifteen of these at least came from Jumièges. Amongst the earliest and most conspicuous of the new foundations was the Conqueror's new abbey on the site of the battle of Hastings at Battle – St Martin de Bello, which was peopled by monks from Marmoutier in the Touraine. New or refoundations in the immediate wake of the Conquest included Chester (directly from Bec, 1093), Selby (1068), Shrewsbury (1085), Colchester (1095) and Tewkesbury (1102). These creations were mostly grafted on to existing settlements and unlike contemporary castles and cathedrals they did not always result in large-scale disturbance to existing town plans. Shrewsbury Abbey, for example, founded by the Earl of Shrewsbury, Roger of Montgomery, lay outside the loop of the River Severn which was occupied by the Saxon town.

In addition to the foundation of a few new abbeys and the refoundation of others, new monastic orders were introduced into England a generation or so after the Conquest. This development started off as a form of French ecclesiastical colonialism, but later blended with the mainstream movement of new monastic foundations found throughout western Europe in the second half of the twelfth century. Many Norman nobles were antipathetic to Saxon Benedictine houses, which were regarded as centres of ideological resistance, and often translated them to the more acceptable Augustinian order. Later, magnates wishing to insure their souls had two alternatives: they could either grant land to Norman monasteries with which they were already associated or they could found new monasteries in England. A Cluniac or Cistercian foundation offered the best of both worlds, enabling them to build a French monastery on English soil.

The first generation of new monks were the Cluniacs, a powerful reformed Benedictine order based at the great mother house of Cluny in Burgundy. The Cluniacs were to have a profound impact politically and ecclesiastically throughout Europe. One of the most influential of the creations in England was the priory founded by Earl William of Warenne and his Flemish wife Gundrada (1078–81) at Lewes in Sussex. Several of the greater French abbeys had received gifts of land and churches in England from the Conqueror, but at first they showed little enthusiasm for setting up dependent houses in a territory they regarded as barbarous and unfriendly. At first, St Hugh of Cluny even refused a request from William to send monks to English abbeys on the grounds that supervision of a distant overseas dependency would be impossible.

The priory of St Pancras at Lewes was the first of thirty-six houses which came to constitute the English province of the Cluniac empire, but the Cluniacs failed to inspire to the same degree in England as they did on the Continent. In no way can the Cluniac houses be thought of as part of a highly organized and centralized order. They varied enormously in

83 A detail from the lavatorium (wash-house) in the cloister at Wenlock Priory, Shropshire. The elegant sculpture is thought to be the work of the Hereford school. (English Heritage)

size and importance, as did the number of people in them; 'the growth was quite haphazard, depending entirely on the accident of gifts of land' (Knowles). Only Wenlock Priory, founded *c*. 1080 (83), Deptford, 1107, and Lewes itself could be said to have been completely successful, although the remains of some Cluniac priories, particularly that at Thetford, form remarkable ruins.

Following the Cluniacs there was a great monastic invasion which continued for a century and a half; 'successive orders like successive tribes and nations crossed the frontiers as if they were impelled by those behind who had come from a greater distance' (Knowles). The greatest impact of all was made by the Cistercians, the white monks. The essence of Cistercian reform was strict observance of the Rule, the restoration of manual work to its place in the monks' day and at first the rejection of such customary sources of income as rents, serfs and churches. The order's most distinctive feature was its strong federal organization based upon a system of affiliation and supervision by a general chapter, which all abbots had to attend annually at Cîteaux in Burgundy. These arrangements

84 The ruined church of the abbey at Buildwas on the banks of the River Severn, close to Ironbridge gorge in Shropshire. The abbey was founded for French monks who became Cistercian in 1147. The simple capitals are typical of Cistercian architecture, but the slightly pointed nature of the nave arches indicates that they date to the latter part of the twelfth century, when the rounded Norman arch was beginning to give way to its Gothic successor. (National Monuments Record)

were set out in the *Carta Caritatis*, the first version of which was composed by Stephen Harding before 1118. The earliest Cistercian plantations were at Waverley (Surrey), 1128, and Rievaulx (Yorks.), 1132. From then onwards the movement spread with phenomenal speed over England and later Wales. Normally their foundations were established in remote and uncultivated districts and in order to facilitate the tasks of clearing forests, draining marshes and overseeing flocks and crops in wild and desolate places, the Cistercians recruited lay brothers from the peasantry on an unprecedented scale (84). In a number of cases the original location of a Cistercian house proved unsatisfactory and the monks moved site. For example, Forde in Dorset was originally founded as a daughter of Waverley at Brightley in Devon, but the community moved first to West Ford and then about 2km (1.5 miles) eastwards to Forde.

The great Cistercian foundations of northern England were also involved in the repopulation process following the Harrying of the North. Some evidence suggests that new Cistercian granges were often established in devastated territory. It is estimated that 44 per cent of all known twelfth-century granges (mainly Cistercian) were built on land that had been completely or largely waste in 1086. Although the Cistercians were at first a simple and solitary order, their buildings were often on a large scale, symbolized by Fountains Abbey in Yorkshire, which today forms the largest monastic ruin in England with a substantially complete claustral nucleus, including a mill, inner gatehouse and remains of inner and outer court buildings set within an extensive walled precinct (85).

In the wake of the Cistercians came the Premonstratensians, who had originated as an

apostolic preaching institution at Prémontré, near Laon in northern France, but under the influence of St Bernard and the Cistercians had become a semi-monastic order with their houses also founded in remote locations. Between 1170 and 1216 over fifteen of their houses were founded in England, few of which have left extensive remains. Bayham (Sussex) is an important and picturesque exception. There were a number of other orders, including the order of Grandmont and the Carthusians, the latter being a strictly enclosed hermit group. Carthusian houses in England were always very small, with the exception of Witham in Somerset, founded in the twelfth century by Henry II in part reparation for the death of Thomas Becket. At Witham isolation was only achieved by moving peasants out of the Forest of Selwood. Like other Carthusian foundations, William had a 'town house' or 'correrie' for lay brothers a kilometre (half a mile) or so away at Witham Friary, where there is still a fine lay brothers' twelfth-century church. The earthwork of the great cloister at Witham Charterhouse can still be seen, but has the remnants of post-medieval gardens superimposed on it.

Initially there were few opportunities for women to take up holy orders: at the time of the

85 The west front of Fountains Abbey (Yorks.), which dates mainly from the twelfth century. Part of the most famous monastic ruins in England. (National Monuments Record)

Conquest there were only nine English nunneries, but by 1125 there were twenty-five. The wealthiest of these was Shaftesbury (Dorset), which like many of its sister houses benefited from the practice of wealthy families giving grants of land to the nunnery in return for accepting their daughters into the community. Sadly little survives of this once great institution. Shaftesbury followed the Benedictine order, but a new order specifically designed for both nuns and canons was created in the twelfth century by Gilbert, a Norman landowner in the south Lincolnshire village of Sempringham, who created the Gilbertine order for women of the district (1131). Gilbert's success created a rare example of an exclusively English monastic foundation. Sempringham was the first of several double houses of this type in north-eastern England. In the immediate post-Conquest period marriage to an English heiress helped a Norman secure possession of her family's lands. Such unions were not always amicable and fears of exploitation led some Englishwomen to take refuge in nunneries 'not for love of the religious life, but from fear of the French'.

As a direct consequence of the crusades, a number of military orders combining monastic and military functions were founded. It was a combination which appealed greatly to Norman society. The largest such order in England was the Knights of the Temple, or the Knights Templar, as they were popularly known. The Knights Templar often built their naves on a circular plan, basing the design on the Church of the Holy Sepulchre at Jerusalem (86). Their principal house in England was the London Temple, which was consecrated in 1185. Shipley in Sussex provides a rare example of an early Knights Templar church and is characterized by its simplicity and starkness of detail.

Lesser priories

Where lesser lords were unable to afford to found an abbey, they often set up modestly sized priories near to their castle or manor house, and persuaded monks to occupy them. For example, Mannasses Arsic, lord of Cogges just outside

86 The circular nave of Holy Sepulchre, Cambridge. The church was built by the 'Fraternity of the Holy Sepulchre' on the model of the Holy Sepulchre Church, Jerusalem, *c.* 1130. It was heavily restored in the nineteenth century.

Witney in Oxfordshire, established a priory cell next to his newly constructed castle in about 1100, and for a while this was the headquarters for all Fécamp Abbey estates in England. Excavations here indicate that the thegn's hall which lay adjacent to the small Saxon church at Cogges was converted into a small, unimposing priory. Tensions developed between the priory and Mannasses' successors as lords of Cogges, as increasingly and typically Fécamp came to view its English cell as a mere estate office, existing less for the maintenance of religious life than for the collection of revenues. Mannasses' heirs also resented his generosity to Fécamp, which placed a powerful alien interest on their doorstep and restricted control of their churches and tithes. A remarkable if somewhat exaggerated insight into the situation is provided by a letter written by one of Fécamp's monks to his abbot in the 1150s. The writer, who had been sent to investigate the state of the English properties, vividly describes the dereliction that confronted him: 'When I arrived at Cogges I found the house empty of goods and full of filth . . . Life itself would be shorter than the tale of woes if I were to recite all the misfortunes of Cogges.' Subsequently the priory seems to have been staffed by only two or three monks and its importance declined after the 1240s, when Fécamp transferred its English affairs to a new estate centre in Sussex. Excavations here show no trace of formal conventual planning and resemble a small manor house more than a monastery. In this respect Cogges is typical of the small English 'alien' priories, and it is not surprising that in the fourteenth century when the Hundred Years War generated anti-French sentiment they were confiscated by the crown.

The proliferation of monastic orders in the twelfth century resulted in the fourth Lateran council (1215) banning the creation of new orders. In future those patrons who wished to endow a monastery had to choose one of the existing orders, but by this time the great age of monastic sponsorship was over and the geography of English monasticism was virtually complete. By the end of the twelfth century there were more than 600 monastic institutions of different orders in England. They possessed considerable amounts of land and wealth and were to remain a major religious, scholarly, educational and economic element throughout the Middle Ages, although their political power was never to be as great as during the century and a half following the Conquest.

All the monasteries which were founded or refounded by the Normans were dissolved by Henry VIII. In most cases the buildings and their contents were dismantled and survive only in the form of majestic ruins as at Fountains or Much Wenlock. Others such as the Cluniac priory at Montacute (founded 1102) have more or less

disappeared altogether, their sites being marked by low earthworks, and in the case of Montacute by a late medieval gatehouse. The English countryside contains a wealth of monastic earthworks marking the sites of former churches, cloisters, gatehouses, fish and mill ponds, precinct boundaries and parks. Some monastic churches were saved; a number, such as that at St Albans, became cathedrals; others such as Tewkesbury (Glos.) and Stogursey (Som.) became parish churches. The church of St Andrew at Stogursey began life as a priory church founded by monks from Lonlay in Normandy in c. 1120. It is a large church with many purely French characteristics such as the carved capitals and remains of an apsidal chancel, with two apsidal side chapels. The survival of churches such as this serves to remind us of the enormity of the loss of fine Norman art and architecture at the time of the break up of the monasteries.

Parish churches

In England the process of parochial organization had started in the late Saxon period, but the majority of parishes were created in the eleventh and twelfth centuries and thousands of parish churches originated at this time. This often involved the subdivision of large *parochiae* which had been based on Saxon minster churches. Many other parish churches evolved from private chapels attached to thegns' houses or manors, but were normally built afresh in the new Romanesque style, when patrons were able to find money for enlarging and enhancing churches they had inherited. The majority of Saxon churches had been of wood and the Normans replaced them with stone buildings.

Parish churches of stone in the new Norman style were built throughout the land. Some Normans who died on campaign wanted their bodies to rest in churches which they had founded or patronized. As they did not indulge in ostentatious tombs, it is as though entire churches were intended to act as their memorials. Their churches marked their status and their families' endowment: through them

87 (a) The Norman font, St Mary's, Luppit (Devon). Such primitive carving, often incorporating Scandinavian or Celtic elements, was a feature of western England in the twelfth century. (National Monuments Record)
(b) The elaborately carved tympanum of Aston Eyre (Salop), showing Christ's entry into Jerusalem. It is believed to be the work of the twelfth-century Hereford school of architecture.

these new men were proclaiming their dominant position just as earlier cultures had used earthen mounds and treasure hoards. In the words of J. F. A. Mason, 'The Norman baronage of the late 11th century was cruel, greedy, proud, domineering, oppressive, class conscious, usually race-conscious, extraordinarily self confident – except on their death beds.'

At the parish church level it is difficult to distinguish between Saxon and Norman work, and it is in this area that the term 'Anglo-Norman architecture' is perhaps best applied. It has recently been suggested that many parish churches which have been dated as pre-Conquest were actually built by local craftsmen in the first half-century of Norman rule. Many of them, such as St Margaret's, Marton (Lincs.), show an intriguing mixture of Saxon and Norman styles. Other such as St Michael Northgate in Oxford could easily have been built either side of the Conquest. The churches were built by the new manorial lord, who normally employed local Saxon craftsmen. Thus the charming little church of Winstone (Glos.) has what seems to be an Anglo-Saxon tower with a very early Norman apsed church. Similarly at Fingest (Bucks.) the space under the Saxon-looking tower seems to have been used as the nave of the church, as at the Saxon church of Barton upon Humber, yet it probably dates from after the Conquest. Such churches often incorporate herring-bone masonry in their walls, a technique normally associated with late Saxon building, but one which continued well after the Conquest and was applied in castles such as Tamworth (Staffs.) and Corfe (Dorset) as well. The carving, particularly in the tympanum or on the font, is often a primitive type such as that over the north doorway of Stoke-sub-Hamdon, Somerset, where the relief sculpture shows the tree of life with birds, a lamb, a cross, and the zodiac signs of Sagittarius and Leo (**87**).

By the 1130s there were radical changes in the plan and architectural details of parish churches. The typical semi-circular apse imported from France disappeared and chancels were built square-ended, while after 1150 arcaded aisles with west towers became increasingly frequent (**88**). The square-ended chancel had been a late Anglo-Saxon tradition, and the disappearance of the apse both in churches and cathedrals has been interpreted as

88 Cropmark of a ploughed-out church at Itteringham (Norfolk), one of many ancient East Anglian churches to have disappeared. The plan of the building with its rectangular nave and apsidal chancel is typical of many simple Norman parish churches. (Norfolk Museums Service)

a triumph of the native custom in England. It is also possible, however, that this change resulted from a change in ritual requiring larger east windows to allow more light into the church. Paradoxically, it tends to be in the poorer and smaller villages that Norman churches survive best, because just as the Normans wished to stamp their hallmark on the communities which they had acquired with the new Romanesque buildings, so too subsequent generations rebuilt parish churches in new styles as and when funds were available. Only in those communities where there was never a fresh injection of money to rebuild all or part of the church does the Norman parish church tend to survive in its entirety. The best examples of complete local Norman churches are to be found isolated in remote spots such as the chapel of the Holy Trinity at Old Bewick (Northd.), Rock (Herefs.) and Heath Chapel (Salop).

7
The Post-Conquest countryside

In Norman England the majority of people lived directly off the land in the countryside. At first sight the Norman impact on the countryside was minimal; for many Englishmen living in villages and hamlets throughout the land, who were not directly affected by the ravages of Norman armies across the countryside, the changes brought about by the Norman Conquest would appear to have been largely cosmetic. It is true that virtually every country dweller would have had a new landlord and that new manors were created within a framework of Norman estates. Consequently everyone's place in society would have been more firmly delineated through the imposition of feudalism, but what other affects did the Conquest have across rural England? We have already seen something of this impact in the spread of monasticism, which led to the transformation of large areas of countryside. Similarly the conversion of some villages into virtual castle fortresses and the creation of many new rural settlements would also have provided dramatic confirmation of the Conquest in some places (**89**), but many of the rural changes would have been subtle and taken many decades to have evolved.

Our picture of the late eleventh-century English countryside is derived largely from the folios of Domesday Book (1086). Historians used to believe that Domesday held the answer to many questions relating to life in late Saxon and early Norman England. However, generations of scholars have wrestled with its

intricate nomenclature and statistics and it is now clear that Domesday Book is an extremely complex document, likened by one historian 'to an abstruse branch of nuclear physics'. It is also clear that the survey is far from complete in its coverage of eleventh-century England. The Domesday commissioners were primarily interested in recording those items that could be taxed for the crown, and there are large gaps in its coverage of many features, such as parish churches. But even allowing for problems of interpretation and omission the survey portrays a countryside full of activity. In addition to arable and pastoral farming, meadow and woodland, there are references to saltworking, coastal and inland fishing, watermills, vineyards and industrial activity. Occasionally, as in the case of Wilcot in the Vale of Pewsey (Wilts.), the cryptic record of Domesday conveys the sense of a pleasingly prosperous settlement, for it was recorded as having *ecclesia nova, domus optima et vinea bona* (a new church, an excellent house and a good vineyard).

By 1086 the Normans had already introduced a new element of local government, in the form of the manor held by the manorial lord. Strictly speaking the term comes from the Latin *manerium*, which is a version of the French *manoir*. The Norman manor was an economic, political and judicial unit. In its basic form the manor consisted of a village, the manor house, lord's house, demesne land (the lord's home farm), the arable, pasture and meadow of the tenants of various status, commonland, woodland and waste. Manors varied considerably in size, although most were compact and easily identifiable units, frequently coextensive with the ecclesiastical parish which the local lord also controlled; others consisted of land spread out in several different villages or in rare cases even in different counties. This manorial structure was used by William to compile a remarkable inventory of his newly won kingdom. The Domesday commissioners collected their description of England shire by shire, hundred by hundred and manor by manor, that is to say geographically. Their clerks then rearranged the material within each shire into the holdings or estates of each tenant in chief.

The Norman village

The history of most English villages begins at the time of the Norman Conquest as the majority of English village-names appear for the first time in Domesday Book and therefore in a literal sense the Conquest marks a historical beginning. However, most of these settlements had been in existence in Anglo-Scandinavian times, and some of them had originated even before that. Domesday Book records something like 10000 places in 1086 and provides us with a rough map of late Saxon and early Norman England. Our understanding of the development of the English village is still imprecise, but it appears that during the later Saxon period, villages were coalescing from a spread of hamlets and isolated farms into the nuclear units of the type that we are familiar with today. This nucleation may have been accelerated by a growing population, but the Norman administration with its strong emphasis on central control probably contributed to the process.

   The Conquest may also have been responsible for the extensive adoption of the open-field system, in which arable land was divided into narrow strips laid out in large open or common fields. The other most obvious signs of this centralizing authority was in the form of the church and manor house or castle, which in very

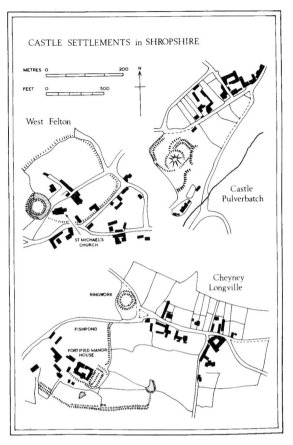

89 Plans of decayed castle settlements in western Shropshire. In all three cases the village plan respects the castle earthworks. At Cheyney Longville the fortified manor house replaced the Norman ringwork to the north.

many villages were built in the hundred or so years after the Conquest. Although there was a good deal of continuity in the location of church sites, there is also some evidence from the excavations of deserted villages to suggest that churches were often located on the sites of peasant houses. Indeed, in the case of Broadfield (Herefs.), the twelfth-century church was sited on peasant crofts which had been destroyed for its construction. The building of the church in this position led to the evolution of a new street plan in the village, aligned on the axis of the church itself. Similar instances of village redesign about this time have been identified elsewhere, for example at the deserted village of Seacourt, on the western edge of Oxford.

As the population grew after the Conquest, so in fertile areas such as East Anglia the land was intensively worked; woodland, fenland and poorer land was also brought into cultivation. In hilly areas the height at which agricultural activity took place rose sharply. On Dartmoor, for instance, there are a large number of deserted villages marking the expansion of agricultural activity in the early Middle Ages. At Hound Tor (Devon), which lies at about 350m (1200ft) above sea level, a number of twelfth-century long-houses have been excavated. Such farmsteads housed humans and animals under the same roof, and were to be found throughout Norman England.

Agricultural expansion was accompanied by new settlements; it has been estimated that in Yorkshire, for example, some 370 places were first recorded between 1067 and 1349. This indicates that one in six of Yorkshire villages came into existence in the post-Conquest era, and some of these were as rigorously planned as contemporary towns. The village of Wheldrake, just outside York, appears to have been laid out between 1066 and 1086, when it consisted of sixteen crofts, eight on each side of the village street. The planning of Wheldrake was associated with woodland clearance. Such regulated villages sometimes appear to have replaced an earlier arrangement of scattered hamlets; for instance, Appleton-le-Moors replaced the two earlier settlements of Appleton and Baschebi. Although such planned villages may have resulted from the Harrying of the North and other acts of scorched earth warfare, they were not restricted to those regions and were commonly located on the estates of high-status landowners such as the Bishop of Durham and the Archbishop of York. Indeed as many as 66 per cent of villages in Durham have regular plans, pointing to a massive programme of village creation and redesign, a programme which some scholars believe may have been well under way at the time of the Conquest (**90**).

Other scholars argue that such planned settlements, which often have standard measurements, were related to early feudal arrangements. It is often difficult to date the origins of these village plans precisely, but the only village of this type to have been excavated, Thrislington (Durham), was laid out before 1200. Although such village redesign is concentrated in northern England, examples are to be found throughout the rest of the country. Excavations at North Elmham (Norfolk) have demonstrated that major changes could occur in a village plan over several hundred years. The succession from mid-Saxon village to episcopal palace in the tenth century was followed by the removal of the manorial buildings, an extension of the cemetery, and a return of village houses to the area in the later tenth century. In the eleventh century there were changes in plan again and also in house types; then in the twelfth century, after the removal of the cathedral to Norwich, a final replanning took place, in which the village was cleared away altogether from the original site to be replaced by a large open green village typically found in East Anglia.

Feudalism

Of all the aspects of the Norman Conquest, it is perhaps feudalism that has been the most problematic and confusing. Conventionally it has been thought that the Normans imposed a completely new system of feudal service on to English society, by which each man held his land from the king in return for the provision of soldiers and military service and that this resulted in a rigidly hierarchical society from the king downwards. It is, however, now quite clear that elements of military service were in place in late Saxon England (see p. 22), but that after the Conquest William imposed a much more systematic arrangement by which each man's obligation was more clearly defined. The baron was granted his estate by the Conqueror, usually consisting of a grouping of lands which had been held by a number of Saxon owners, and in return he owed service of a stated number of knights to the crown. The institution of knight service was introduced from Normandy, but it was not until 1166 that there was a clear statement of feudal

90 Appleton-le-Moors (Yorks.), showing the regulated settlement typical of villages which were laid out afresh after the Harrying of the North. The plan, with its central axial road, parallel property boundaries and back-lanes, is virtually indistinguishable from those of contemporary new towns. (Cambridge University Collection of Air Photographs)

obligations in England, and by this time knights' service had begun to fragment and to be commuted for a money payment.

These developments brought about changes both in the range of titles used and in the status of the holders of those Saxon titles which did survive. There was a radical shake-up in the hierarchical order; for instance, earls, who were the most powerful men in pre-Conquest England, virtually lost all their responsibility and were relegated largely to honorific positions, losing their power to the county sheriffs. Similarly, the Saxon rank of 'thegn', which was to all intents and purposes the lord of the manor, lost any connotation of rank after the Conquest. Conversely the status of the knight rose considerably and a clear social distinction developed between knight and freemen. Not that we should see Norman feudalism introduced at a stroke: it was imposed slowly and erratically and England was never totally feudalized, but the foundations of the system were well established before William's death. Feudalism can be seen as a policy by which William and his successors tried to impose a rigid social structure through which they could implement the claim that all the land of England was the king's, and the king's alone, but it was never totally effective and there was much variation in its application.

Slavery

In late Saxon England there was a ceremonial of servitude, in which the slave placed his head into his lord's (and lady's) hands and was given an ox-goad or a bill-hook, representing the driving of animals and the clearing of land. In 1102 Archbishop Anselm issued a decree against 'that shameful trading' whereby men were 'sold like brute beasts'. Less than two decades earlier Domesday Book had recorded that at Lewes the market toll on the sale of a man was 4d., while that of a horse was 1d. and an ox ½d. Slaves, both male and female, were recorded in England in the late eleventh century, with the highest concentration being in the western counties, where William of Poitiers observed that Gallic peoples customarily sold their captives into slavery. Also the large estates of the West lent themselves to slavery, and in Devon as many as 28 per cent of the population on the estates of Queen Matilda were slaves in 1086.

One rather surprising result of the Conquest was that the Normans abolished the rank of slave. Although slaves had featured in the early history of the Duchy of Normandy, slavery had more or less disappeared there by the time of the Conquest and the great slave market at Rouen is last heard of in about 1000. In England men and women could still be held as chattels and the Domesday Book records that up to 12 per cent of the population in 1086 were slaves. There were several slave markets in England, perhaps the best known being at Bristol, which carried out a thriving trade with Ireland, yet by the end of the twelfth century slaves had virtually disappeared from the records. There was a significant drop in the number of recorded slaves between 1066 and 1086. There is evidence of the emancipation of slaves at Hailes (Glos.), where it was recorded that there were twelve *servi* whom an Englishman, William Leofric, made free. Nevertheless, as late as the 1120s an Anglo-Norman church was able to decree reduction in status to slavery as a suitable punishment for clerical concubines. It was perhaps because the Norman lord regarded all his tenants as his men

and that he had rights in all the persons on his lands that the formal category of slavery had become less important. The tendency was for the peasantry to be characterized as *villeins* or *villani*, which probably reflected the diminished status of most agricultural workers. Indeed, the principal characteristics of a freeman, the right to bear arms and the right to testify on oath in public courts, also diminished in status under Norman feudalism.

Village buildings

There is no evidence to suggest that there was any significant change in the form of village houses during the immediate post-Conquest period, although the manor house and manor farm assumed a greater significance in the village than their Saxon predecessors. Excavations at Goltho (Lincs.) demonstrate in a very dramatic way the changes between a late Saxon thegn's house and a Norman manor, and how such a building could develop through the twelfth to thirteenth centuries. At Goltho the manorial establishment comprised a substantial hall, which was rebuilt several times in the tenth and eleventh centuries, together with an area defined by a simple boundary bank and ditch, which was not defensive. When the Normans came in the second half of the eleventh century the position was radically changed by the building of a defensive ringwork with a large bank and ditch within which there was a smaller hall and a defensive tower. The farm buildings would have been built in an outer enclosure and so separated off from the main living accommodation. The difference between life under the Norman lord and that under the Saxon thegn living in his hall, set in the middle of farm buildings, bounded only by a slight earthwork, is demonstrated here. When, after 1066, an alien lord took up residence among a potentially hostile population, the living and farm activities were separated from one another and the Norman lord was set apart in a defended enclosure. When in the twelfth century times became more settled and relations between seigneur and peasant became more normal, the ringwork was levelled to form a platform for a large aisled hall. Within the ditch there was only room for the hall, kitchen and another small building; therefore with the need for a larger, more compact establishment in the thirteenth century the manor was moved about half a mile to a new site to the south where a moated manorial complex was constructed.

In troubled areas and troubled times, lords often built their manor houses in the form of castles. For example, virtually every village on the border between England and Wales boasts a Norman manorial fortification. Castles were often physically imposed on villages in much the same way that they were built in towns. During the Anarchy, for instance, a castle was built at Eaton Socon (Beds.) which sealed a late Saxon church and cemetery together with other village buildings. More often than not such early rural castles were built in earth and timber, but a few were built of stone and survive in modified form as fortified manor houses. Such fortified manors were sometimes seen as a demonstration of status, an alternative to which was a stone-built manor, a few of which survive as at Boothby Pagnell (Lincs.) (**91**). Here the exterior arches of the lower storey reflect its use for storage. Inside there are plain stone walls with a splendid rib-vaulted undercroft over the room on one side and a vault on the other. The entrance to the first-floor living hall is by way of an external stone stairway. Another rare example of a late Norman manor house is at Saltford, near Keynsham (Som.), built about 1150. Again, this building has an upper-floor hall and solar with a service area on the ground floor. Other surviving examples of Norman stone manor houses are at Hemingford Grey Manor (Hunts.), Port Slade Manor (Sussex), Burton Agnes Old Manor (Yorks.), and Charleston Manor (Sussex).

When it comes to examining lesser village houses there are problems, since no Norman houses of this type survive above ground, as in most cases they were too flimsy to survive. The pattern of constant rebuilding makes it almost impossible to obtain earlier village plans in surviving villages as the remains are either covered by standing buildings or have been destroyed or seriously disturbed over the centuries. Analysis is therefore possible only on deserted village sites where medieval levels have not been disturbed by later activity. Even on these sites the plans of earlier structures are complicated by later disturbances. Excavation over the past thirty years has produced evidence of three basic house types and a development from primitive to more sophisticated timber-framed or stone-built houses. At Goltho (Lincs.) we are fortunate in having a picture of the development of early medieval peasant houses in the same way as we have for the manorial complex at the same site. The earliest peasant houses in a single toft were first of all constructed of clay in the eleventh and twelfth centuries without any posts penetrating into the ground. Later in the twelfth and early thirteenth

91 Interior doorway of the Norman manor house at Boothby Pagnell (Lincs.). (National Monuments Record)

centuries the houses were defined by post-holes. In the early periods it is hard to define the nature of the buildings and the use of the various rooms, though one early house was a small long-house in which animals were kept in the lower end. Each house was built in a new position, not overlapping the earlier foundations as was often the case on sites such as Wharram Percy (Yorks.). Excavated artefacts from Norman village sites show little change from the Saxon period, although the range and sophistication of domestic artefacts, particularly in relation to dress, becomes greater in the second half of the twelfth century. The range of pottery forms also becomes greater and there is evidence of imported wares being brought into eastern England. In many western parts of England locally fired pottery makes a reappearance at this stage after being absent for several centuries.

Norman place-names

As the Norman Conquest did not involve a large-scale movement of French-speaking peoples into England, it did not bring about a complete change in the vernacular language from Saxon to French, although after 1066 English was heavily influenced by French. The Dialogue of the Exchequer, written late in the twelfth century, declared that English and Norman were so intermingled that 'it can scarcely be discerned at the present day – who is English and who is Norman by race', and indeed eventually the descendants of the Norman aristocracy spoke English, not French. French had relatively little impact on place-names compared to those languages which had been introduced by Saxon and Scandinavian peasant settlers. Nevertheless, place-name scholars have shown ways in which the coming of the Normans considerably modified the spelling of many English place-names, reflecting the way in which French-speaking clerks rendered the pronunciation of English country people. The influence of Norman scribes is very strong in Domesday Book and in official records of the twelfth century. When they

came across sounds or combinations of sounds which were absent from French or Latin they would tend to substitute for them the nearest sounds in those languages; a common example of Norman influence is the substitution of *c* for *ch* in names such as Towcester (Northants) and Cerne (Dorset). Similarly, *T* often replaced *Th* as in Tingrith (Beds.) and Tinsmore (Oxon.) and *J* replaced *G* as in Jarrow (Dur.) and Jevington (Sussex).

A few villages adopted completely French names, but wholesale changes from a Saxon or Scandinavian name to a French one are rare. Exceptions are to be found in places where there was a new settlement, abbey or castle. For example, the Saxon place-name Sheene was replaced by Richmond ('strong hill'), Biscopestone by Montacute ('pointed hill'), and Tattershall by Pontefract ('broken bridge'). There are several place-names that incorporate descriptive adjectives such as *beau* or *bel*, such as Belsize ('beautiful sea'), Beaulieu ('beautiful place'), Beaumont ('beautiful hill') and Beaudesert ('beautiful wilderness'). One exception was Beaumont in Essex, which replaced the old Saxon name of Fulanpettae (old English for 'foul pit'). A few places were given names incorporating the element *mal* ('poor' or 'bad'). Kirkby Malzeard (Yorks.) comes from 'mal assart', and Malpass, which occurs at least eight times in England and Wales, usually refers to marshy grounds, but such disparaging Norman place-names are unusual, or at least relatively few of them have survived.

Norman personal names were sometimes attached to an earlier Saxon place-name element. The largest single group was compounded with old English *ton* ('farmstead', 'village') in names such as Williamston (Northd.). Some names are of Breton origin, such as Wigan (Lancs.), while others like Lambin (Cumbd.) are Flemish, indicating the presence of Bretons and Flemings among the new post-Conquest settlers. The name Flimsby (Cumbd.) actually means 'the village of the Flemings'. There are also a considerable number of village-names where a

French family name has been attached to an old English settlement-name providing us with some of our more exotic and bizarre place-names, for example, Stoke Mandeville, Bury Pomeroy, Combe D'Abitot and Shepton Mallet. Occasionally, the names have blended as in the case of Stokesay (Salop), which comes from the English word Stoke, meaning 'mother church', and the family name of de Say, or Stogursey (Som.), which is an Anglicized form of Stoke de Courcy. Villages given to Norman abbeys after the Conquest sometimes adopted the name of the mother house, as was the case with Tooting Bec (Surrey) and Weedon Bec, both of which belonged to the abbey of Bec.

Royal Forests

> With the kingdom made safe on all sides . . . the most kindly Edward passed his life in security and peace, and spent much of his time in the glades and woods in the pleasures of hunting. After divine service, which he gladly and devoutly attended every day, he took much pleasure in hawks and birds of that kind which were brought before him, and was really delighted by the baying and scrambling of the hounds

observed Edward the Confessor's monk chronicler. The Saxon kings had hunted and created game reserves specifically for that purpose, but these were not forests in the legal sense. The Saxons actually had no word for 'forest', although the concept of the king's wood was not a new one. Kingswood in the Kentish Weald, for example, was so called from the mid-Saxon period onwards, and specific areas such as Woodstokechase in Oxfordshire were associated with the hunting activities of the Saxon kings.

The Norman kings' preoccupation with hunting was legendary, and William, it is said, 'loved the stags as much as if he were their father'. Forest law represented one of the major legal innovations which the Normans introduced into England and imposed specific laws on royal hunting areas. 'Forest' was a legal term applied to land governed by forest laws designed for the protection of deer and where only the monarch could hunt. It was not until 1184 that the first Forest Act, known as 'The Assize of Woodstock', was passed, but this appears to have been composite legislation restating practices that had been gradually adopted since the Conquest. Forest law included the right to keep deer, to appoint forest officials, to hold forest courts and to levy fines. At one stage in the twelfth century up to a third of England was Royal Forest, and forest law became increasingly restrictive. It was only in 1216 that the crown, unable to withstand the antagonism which the laws generated, began to loosen its legal hold on the forests. William and his successors had transported the forest law and forest courts of Normandy to England. These had originally derived from Carolingian imperial law and were introduced to service the rapid, and at times violent, extension of forest land. At the time of William's death in 1087 only about a quarter of Royal Forests had been created, and many forests, such as Epping (1130) and Sherwood (1154), are not heard of until the twelfth century (**92**).

The creation of a forest, particularly the New Forest, created a deep impression upon the minds of contemporaries; and antagonism to the Royal Forest system may have caused their impact to be greatly exaggerated. John of Worcester alleged that William I had depopulated a fruitful and prosperous countryside and destroyed houses and churches to make way for the deer, so that popular rumour declared that the death of William Rufus, while he was hunting in the New Forest, was an act of divine retribution for the impious act of his father. But modern scholarship suggests that the Norman and Angevin kings tended to impose forest laws mainly upon districts where clearing and cultivation had made comparatively slow progress because of the unfavourable terrain. For the most part Royal Forests were not physically demarcated on the ground, although physical features such as rivers and hills were used as boundaries and occasionally linear banks and ditches were dug to

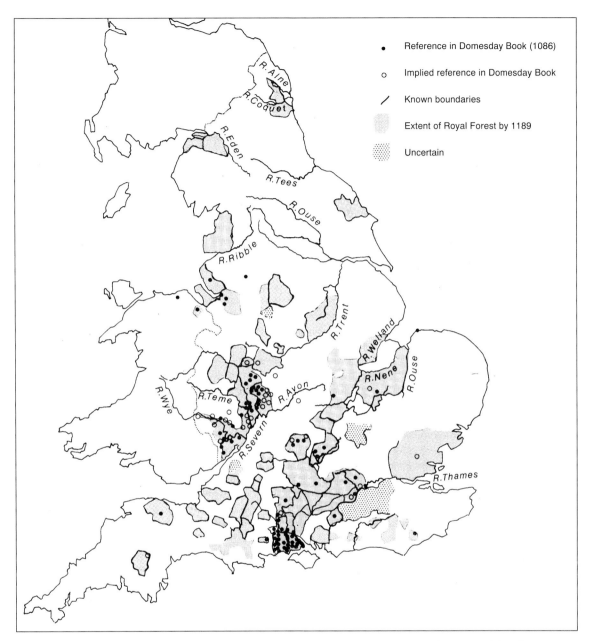

92 Map of the Royal Forests of England in the twelfth century. (Judith Dobie)

delineate the forest edge. In 1280 the 'metes and bounds' of the New Forest were said 'to extend from the Test westwards to the Avon, and from the Solent northwards to the Wiltshire county boundary'.

By the early thirteenth century references to activities other than hunting within the forests are common. In 1237 the Constable of St Briavels was ordered to 'cause to be erected nine mobile underwood forges' and 'to sustain those forges . . . with thorn, maple, hazel and other underwood; so that no oak, chestnut or beech be cut down and to cause the area fell and allocated to be well and sufficiently fenced lest any deer or other beast be able to get in to browse there'. In 1228 the king ordered a forester in Hainault Forest 'to make a certain lime kiln for works of the said Tower of London', and the provision of timber for royal castles and palaces was an important function of the forest from the late eleventh century onwards.

Henry II enthusiastically extended the Royal Forests, which were at their most extensive in the late twelfth century. But by the mid-thirteenth century, when records of individual forests become plentiful, they were already in decline. The crown turned the process of disafforestation into a source of revenue. For example, in 1204 the Men of Cornwall agreed to pay 2000 marks and five palfreys for the disafforestation of the whole of the county and in the same year the Men of Essex paid 500 marks and five palfreys for the disafforestation of Essex north of the 'Stanestreet'. Although the process of disafforestation was a protracted one extending over hundreds of years, the true Royal Forests were a relatively short-lived feature of the English landscape. Only the early medieval kings at the very height of their authority were able to impose and maintain such a system, and thus the forest should be seen very much as a characteristic of Norman England.

Chases and parks

Although in theory only the crown could control forests, there were large areas which were operated by private individuals on the basis of Royal Forest. The forest was the supreme status symbol for aristocratic families, such as those of the Earls of Richmond and the Bishops of Durham and Winchester. In Cheshire the Forests of Wirral, Delamere, Mondrum and Macclesfield were all in the hands of earls. Throughout the Middle Ages the term 'chase' is inconsistently used to distinguish the forest of a private subject from that of the crown. Normally, chases and parks were carved out of woodland or moor, but in some instances their creation involved the expropriation of agricultural land. In the mid-twelfth century, for instance, in the North Riding of Yorkshire, William Le Gros destroyed several villages to create a chase.

It would appear from some entries in Domesday Book that there were enclosures for the retention of animals in Saxon England; these were recorded as 'hays' in Domesday Book. Some thirty-five parks of woodland beasts are mentioned and topographical evidence of places such as Great Ongar (Essex) shows the presence of pre-Conquest parks. However, in general park creation seems to have been a feature of post-Conquest feudal England and the crown held parks both within and outside areas of Royal Forest. The earliest Norman parks appear to have been in the south-east and eastern part of the country. Five parks in Sussex are mentioned in Domesday Book and by 1145 the lords of all the Sussex rapes held parks, mostly adjacent to their castles.

The medieval park differed from the forest and chase in that it was normally defined by a boundary consisting of a ditch and wooden pale or in certain areas a stone wall. The royal parks of Devizes and Woodstock were enclosed by stone walls. The expense of maintaining these enclosures was nominally met by the crown, but in the case of Northampton Park, nearby tenants owed the labour service of repairing specified lengths of the park boundary. Most medieval parks have subsequently been cleared and enclosed for agriculture or incorporated in larger landscaped parks. Their linear earthworks survive in the landscape today, and place-names such as Park Farm and Park End or Lodge often provide an indication of the site of a former park. The parks were essentially for the retention of deer, at first roe and red deer, but later exclusively fallow deer (**93**).

Similarly Nottingham and Guildford had parks adjacent to them in the twelfth century. At Devizes, Bishop Roger of Salisbury created a park adjacent to his new castle and castle town and created a classic example of Norman seigneurial landscape design as the large ovoid-shaped park to the west mirrors exactly the shape of the town and castle to the east. The parks were another demonstration of Norman superiority and domination. In the words of Professor Maurice Beresford, 'if the seigneur of Devizes looked westward from his ramparts he saw his pallisaded deer park and if eastward the burgage plots, market place and church of his castle borough'. At Clipston in Sherwood Forest the crown spent over £500 on the

building of a chamber and chapel, the construction of a fish pond and the formation of the deer park.

Interest in hunting, however, was not restricted to deer in Norman England. The rabbit, a Norman introduction, was encouraged, and rabbit warrens were often deliberately created within deer parks. The pillow mounds found on Dartmoor and other moorland areas were created for rabbits, and a charter issued to

93 Plan showing the distribution of deer parks in eastern England. (Judith Dobie)

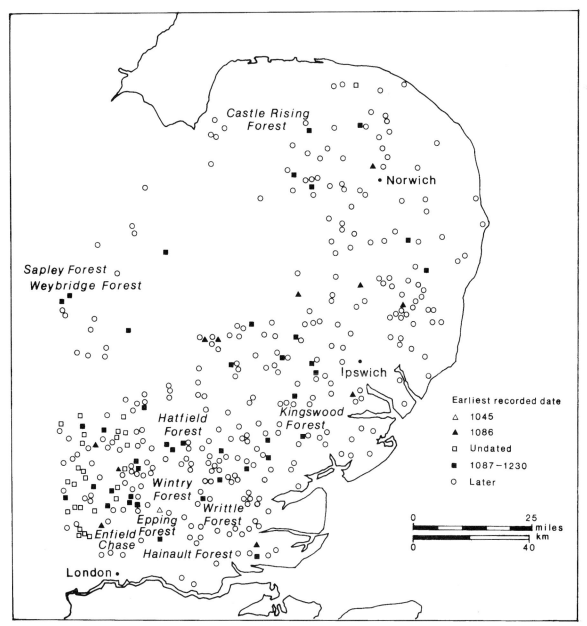

Earliest recorded date

△   1045
▲   1086
□   Undated
■   1087–1230
○   Later

Tavistock Abbey by Henry I, for example, authorized the abbot to maintain rabbit warrens. Domesday Book includes some reference to hawks' nests, mainly in the Welsh Marches, confirming that falconry like hunting was a favoured sport of Anglo-Norman kings and aristocracy. Other means of retaining and breeding birds and fish became an integral part of the manorial economy in the twelfth century, when dovecotes and fishponds were established throughout the country, and whose remains can still be identified in the form of earthworks or place-names and occasionally standing structures. Much survives in the modern landscape as a reminder of the forests and deer parks. The remains of the former royal hunting palaces, where the monarch could conduct affairs of state as well as indulge in the chase, can be found at Bagden Lodge in Savernake Forest and Grovely Lodge near Wilton. Little remains of the most important of all such forest palaces, at Clarendon, whose park was more than 5km (3 miles) in diameter. Many deer

parks with their great banks and ditches are still deeply embedded in the landscape and have influenced road patterns, field shapes and place-names. They vary in size from just a few acres as at Middleton Stoney (Oxon.) to the three thousand acres of Windsor Great Park.

Woodstock Park

In the case of Woodstock (Oxon.) we have more information about a park which was founded before the Conquest. Ethelred II held a council at Woodstock on the land of the Mercians and there is a brief reference in Domesday Book to

94 The western boundary of Blenheim Park, Woodstock (Oxon.). The area was established as a royal hunting area, and Domesday Book records that Woodstock was part of an extensive tract of 'demesne forest' in north Oxfordshire. It is probable that Henry I made the first enclosure of the park in the first half of the twelfth century. The park pale was seen in the form of a bank and ditch which enabled deer to enter the park area, but prevented them from leaving.

the extent of the king's demesne forests of Woodstock, Cornbury and Wychwood. It is recorded that Henry I came here on many occasions and that it was 'the favourite seat of his retirement and privacy'. A grant of Abingdon Abbey, which is dated 1110, was signed 'at Woodstock in the park', and according to later accounts it was in this or the following year that Henry I enclosed the park with a stone wall (94). There are frequent references during the twelfth century to work on the wall, and in 1164–5, for example, £30 was spent on its maintenance. Henry of Huntingdon refers to Woodstock as 'a remarkable place which he had made a dwelling-place for men and beasts' and William of Malmesbury elaborated on this by describing 'a park called Woodstock' in which the king kept wild animals, brought from abroad, including a porcupine sent to him by William of Montpelier. Within the park there appears to have been a menagerie as well as water gardens, fish ponds, and later pavilions. Later records reveal that 'King Henry II visited the manor house of Woodstock for love of a certain woman called Rosamund' and go on to tell of the creation of a new town here, probably in the

years 1174–6; 'And there was a waste place without the said park and manor and because men lodged too far, the king gave places to diverse men to build hostelries there for the use of the King's men.'

It is clear from later documents that Woodstock Park was much more exotic than the average deer park. It had a royal palace, gardens and pavilions, some of which in the Moorish style used water as a principal design element. The water gardens were centred around a spring known as Everswell, later called Rosamund's Bower. It has been suggested that the gardens here were inspired by the twelfth-century romance of *Tristan and Isolde*, a version of which was probably written for Henry II. The most likely source of inspiration, however, was Sicily, where the Norman kings had a series of rural pavilions within easy reach of their capital at Palermo, and one of these, the Palace of La Zisa, had a central court across which water from a spring ran through a series of basins set in the floor, a device which the Normans had borrowed from the Moslems. Everswell now lies under the lake, which forms one of the principal features of Capability Brown's later landscaping of Blenheim Park.

Epilogue: the Norman legacy

War was of central significance to Anglo-Norman society, and the most obvious legacy of the Norman conquest of England is to be found in the buildings and earthworks of castles, cathedrals, abbeys and churches. These edifices were the imperial tools and symbols of conquest and characterized the difference between earlier Scandinavian and Anglo-Saxon colonization. Nothing like them had been seen since the Roman conquest of Britain in the first century AD, and the sheer extent of building and rebuilding was not to be seen on the same scale in England again until the industrial era. The fact that the Normans were eventually assimilated into English society makes the task of evaluating their contribution more difficult, and paradoxically while evidence of the Normans is found everywhere on the grand scale, at the local level many aspects of life remained unaltered. Some scholars argue that the chief characteristics of Anglo-Norman society were in place before the Conquest, but that it was the Conquest which defined them more precisely. Many of the changes that followed in the century and a half after 1066 were subtle and can only be detected through the archaeological and historical record.

Yet 1066 was also a real watershed. It was the last time that England was successfully invaded and conquered. It was marked by a total change of land ownership and it established the basis on which England became an important and from time to time dominant player on the European scene. Before 1066 the English kings had played a distinguished role on the fringes of Christendom, but after the Conquest their Norman successors became rulers of continental importance. In the past it has been customary to attribute much of this success to the mysterious quality of Norman feudalism, but the strength of the old English administrative system lay with its local institutions and by imposing royal supervision on this system the Norman monarchy was able to blend local society, in the lay lords, the Church and royal administration, into one. William started a process which culminated under Henry I and Henry II, who, more than any of their contemporaries in Europe, were real masters of all the people of their lands. It was the combination of elements from both English and Frankish society that created this unique manifestation of royal power.

Places to visit

There are numerous sites, buildings and monuments in England which incorporate Norman remains. Many parish churches contain elements of Norman architecture, although very few eleventh- and twelfth-century buildings survive in their entirety. Nevertheless, even the most unlikely Victorian-looking churches can contain a Norman gem in the form of a font or tympanum.

It is impossible in the space available to provide a comprehensive list of places to visit. I have therefore chosen a representative sample, which to me reflects Norman England. Foremost among these is, of course, Battle in Sussex.

Battle Abbey

The abbey was founded on the site of the battle of Hastings soon after 1066. Only a little of the original Norman monastery survives, although the outline of the church is described on the ground, and part of the medieval abbey has been converted into a school. The site of the battle lies to the south of the abbey and remains as open fields. There is an English Heritage trail which allows one to walk through the battlefield, although there are few obvious surviving landmarks apart from the general terrain, which gives a good impression of how the battle was fought. To the north of the abbey lies the planned town of Battle, which was created soon after the abbey was founded.

Berkhamsted Castle (Herts.)

The site where the English eventually surrendered to William is marked by a motte and bailey castle, probably erected by William's half-brother, Robert of Mortain. Today the castle is surrounded by intrusive roads, but the earthworks here are still worth a visit, with a dominant motte and an oblong bailey. The surviving masonry dates in part to the time when the castle was under the stewardship of Thomas Becket.

Castle Acre (Norfolk)

Castle Acre has an assemblage of Norman ruins and buildings. It consists of the castle, the attached defended town and the Cluniac priory. The castle was founded soon after the Conquest by the Warenne earls of Surrey. Its principal building was what could now be termed a country house, but in the twelfth century the castle defences were greatly strengthened and a remarkable construction of the original house took place, turning it into a keep. In the fourteenth century the castle appears to have fallen into disuse, and much of its flint stonework was removed by stone-robbers, partly to provide domestic dwellings in the town. A little to the west of the town, William de Warenne's son founded a wealthy and imposing Cluniac priory about 1090. The west front of the church here, with its blind arcading, is one of the marvels of Norman architecture in England.

Castle Rising (Norfolk)

The great palace castle keep at Castle Rising sits within a monumental earthwork of Norman date. The keep was built c. 1140 by William Albini II to celebrate his marriage to the widow of Henry I and consequent acquisition of the earldom of Sussex. It was modelled on the keep at Norwich and was amongst the largest and most ornate in the kingdom, particularly important for its richly decorated forebuilding, and the staircase approach to it. The remains of a Norman church which reuses Roman material also lies within the earthwork.

Conisbrough Castle (S. Yorks.)

This is the late Norman nobleman's castle par excellence, built by Hamelin Plantagenet, Henry II's half-brother. It has a round keep dating to about 1180 with extraordinary powerful buttresses around it containing a chapel and various other chambers. The stonework is of fine quality. It occupies a dominant site in an otherwise built-up area.

Dover Castle (Kent)

Apart from the Tower of London, Dover Castle is the major Norman castle of England. There was probably a wooden structure here until 1168, when Henry II decided to guard the Channel. The huge tower-keep was completed in 1184, with its inner curtain wall and eleven turrets, the first such in Europe.

Durham Cathedral (Co. Durham)

This is the great masterpiece of Norman cathedrals, rebuilt from 1093 onwards as the major religious centre for the North, and is probably the most complete Norman cathedral in England. Adjacent to the cathedral is the castle mound, attached to which are a number of Norman features, including parts of Framwellgate Bridge, built in 1128 by Bishop Flambard.

Fountains Abbey (N. Yorks.)

Fountains Abbey is the most complete Cistercian monastery to have survived. It was founded in 1132; much of it was built during the twelfth century, and it incorporates extensive Norman architectural remains, complete with cloister. A Benedictine nunnery was founded here originally in the seventh century, and refounded in 1120. There is an almost complete church of c. 1160 with a splendid triple-arched doorway.

Holy Trinity near Byers (Cambs.)

Norman main chancel plus a tower of c. 1200 with considerable zig-zag decoration and arcading both inside and out.

Kilpeck Church (Hereford & Worcester)

Kilpeck Church is the best surviving work of the celebrated Herefordshire school of Norman architecture. The west windows, the corbel-tables and particularly the south doorway and the chancel arch are decorated with intricately twining trails and figures, and many other delicately executed motifs. In the field beside the church, to the west, is the castle, of which mainly earthworks survive. To the east lies a rectangular enclosure in which lay a settlement, possibly a former borough.

Kirkstall (W. Yorks.)

Extensive ruins of the twelfth-century Cistercian priory. The impressive ruins show buildings mostly of c. 1155–75. The church is still a simple Cistercian plan.

Launceston Castle (Cornwall)

Launceston Castle is mainly thirteenth century, and was built on the site of a motte and bailey by Robert Mortain. The round shell keep dates to about 1200. Nearby, the church of St Thomas has a strange Norman font and tympanum.

Lincoln

Lincoln has probably the best surviving group of Norman vernacular buildings in England, with the Norman house of c. 1170–80, the Jew's house of the same date with original windows and chimney breast and St Mary's Guild of 1180–90 juxtaposing stone frontage windows and doors and a large courtyard entrance arch.

Lindisfarne (Northd.)

Although the site on Holy Island is best known for the Celtic monastery founded from Iona by St Aidan in 635, the ruins here are those of the great Benedictine priory of *c.* 1110–40. The nave is particularly fine, with eroded drum piers in the Durham style.

Ludlow (Shropshire)

Ludlow was a post-Conquest town, starting life in the form of a broad market place running to the east of the stone gatehouse built by Roger de Lacy *c.* 1085. Later the town was laid out in a regular grid. Within the original bailey a chapel with a circular nave was built in the mid-twelfth century; it survives as only one of four such circular churches in England.

Melbourne (Derby.)

The three-tower church of St Michael and Mary is dominated by a splendid six-bay aisled nave with drum piers and stilted arches. Much of the church dates between 1135 and 1150.

Milton St Andrew (Dorset)

Beautifully decorated flint-built Norman church.

Norham Castle (Northd.)

The Bishop of Durham's curved three-storey hall keep, *c.* 1160, overlooks the River Tweed, which here forms the Scottish border. This remarkable castle is perhaps one of the best in the whole of England, but is little visited. At the other end of the town is a Norman church, much of which dates to the late twelfth century. Between the two in typical fashion is a broad market square, which probably dates to the late Middle Ages.

Norwich (Norfolk)

Norwich is perhaps the most Norman of English towns, with its splendid cathedral and castle. The cathedral was started in 1096 after the

bishop's seat moved here from North Elmham via Thetford. The nave, started in 1115–20, has massive spiral Durham-type carved drum piers, and was completed by 1145. The west front is Norman, with many alterations. The castle consists of a large rectangular hall keep *c.* 1160 with complex blank arcaded walls on a purlieu of mortar. It was restored to its original design in 1833 by Salvin.

Old Sarum (Wilts.)

Just north of Salisbury lies an Iron Age hillfort, later fortified by the Romans and Saxons. It is the place where William the Conqueror inspected his victorious army in 1170. The Normans built a castle and cathedral at Old Sarum under the control of the bishops of Salisbury. Later they moved to New Sarum (Salisbury), where the great Gothic cathedral was erected in the thirteenth century.

Pevensey (Sussex)

William landed at Pevensey Bay early in the morning on 20 September 1066 with his invading force and camped within the fort which had been built by the Romans as a defence against Germanic raiders in the third and fourth centuries AD. After the Conquest, William gave the fortification to his half-brother Robert of Mortain, who built a keep on the eastern side of the enclosure. Along with the site of the battle of Hastings, Pevensey provides perhaps one of the most poignant landmarks in the story of the Norman Conquest in England.

Richmond (N. Yorks.)

The town of Richmond has been dominated by Alan the Red's castle for nine centuries. Rufus, son of the Count of Penthièrre, began the building in 1071 having been given the land by William the Conqueror. Richmond is one of the few English castles to have surviving eleventh-century walls. It maintains the original gateway within the keep. The remains of the original hall in the south corner are a rare example of surviving Norman domestic architecture.

Southall Minster (Notts.)

The minster is one of the glories of Norman architecture on the grand scale. The Norman collegiate church was founded in 1108. The nave transepts and crossing date to the first half of the twelfth century. With its west towers and pyramidal roofs and central tower, the minster church provides a model of Norman ecclesiastical architecture. The canons of Southall Minster owned a quarter of Nottinghamshire up to the Reformation.

Tewkesbury Abbey (Glos.)

Tewkesbury Abbey is one on the great Norman Benedictine churches built from 1087 onwards and is one of the relatively few monastic churches to survive the dissolution of the monasteries as it became the parochial church for the town.

Totnes (Devon)

Unusually, two of the original Norman gates survive in Totnes. Totnes Castle was founded by Judhael, a Breton, who supported Robert, the Conqueror's eldest son, against Rufus. The original motte and bailey survive, and there is a shell keep about 20m (70ft) in diameter. The shape of the whole town is dictated by the castle and the ancient core site within an extended outer bailey.

Waltham Abbey

The church of Waltham Abbey lies on the site of King Harold's abbey and dates to *c.* 1060. The Norman nave of *c.* 1120 survives with Durham-type drum piers incised with spirals. Waltham was Harold's holy place, where he enshrined a piece of the holy cross found uncovered at Montacute in Somerset. It was here that Harold's body was eventually laid to rest.

Wenlock Priory (Shropshire)

The ruins of the Cluniac priory at Much Wenlock incorporate some fine ornate blind arcading in the chapter house and impressive figure sculpture in the lavatorium dating to about 1180. The priory is believed to be the work of the Herefordshire school of architecture.

The White Tower (Tower of London)

The White Tower, the Tower of London, is probably the best-known Norman building in England. It consists of a four-storey hall-keep, with main hall and many apartments and galleries dating from *c.* 1078–97. The curved projection on the east contains the chapel of St John. Norman masonry is to be found beside the keep and elsewhere, but the curtain walls were started after 1200. The Tower was probably the strongest Norman building in England, and declared London to be the capital of William's newly won realm.

Winchester Cathedral and Wolvesey Palace (Hants)

Winchester was the capital of Alfred and his Wessex dynasty of kings of England. Work on the Norman cathedral started in 1070, but only the groin vaulted crypt and the north and south transepts of *c.* 1090 survive. The rest of the immense cathedral was rebuilt in Gothic. The monks of the priory of St Swithin erected the longest church in Christendom, 170m (555ft) long. To the east of the cathedral are the remains of Wolvesey Palace, built by the prince-bishop Henry of Blois, providing a fitting monument to the power of the twelfth-century Norman bishops. The Norman church was built in the shape of a cross by Henry as a hospital for thirteen poor men 'feeble and so reduced in strength so they could hardly, or with difficulty, support themselves without another's aid'. The oldest part is the choir of *c.* 1150, which is generally regarded as one of the finest examples of Norman transitional in the country.

Further reading

1 General

Allen Brown, R., *The Normans* (London: Guild Publishing, 1984)

Barlow, F., *William Rufus* (London: Methuen, 1983)

Bates, D., *Normandy Before 1066* (London: Longman, 1982)

Brown, A., *Anglo-Norman Studies: Proceedings of the Battle Conference on Anglo-Norman Studies*, 1–4 (1979–82), continued from 1983 as *Anglo-Norman Studies* (Woodbridge: The Boydell Press, 1979–)

Campbell, J. (ed.), *The Anglo-Saxons* (Oxford: Phaidon, 1982)

Chibnall, M., The *World of Orderic Vitalis* (Oxford: OUP, 1984)

Chibnall, N., *Anglo-Norman England: 1066–1166* (Oxford: Blackwell, 1986)

Clarke, H., *The Archaeology of Medieval England* (Oxford: Blackwell, 1984)

Davis, R. H. C., *The Normans and their Myth* (London: Thames & Hudson, 1968)

Davis, R. H. C., *From Alfred the Great to Stephen* (Woodbridge: The Hambledon Press, 1991)

Holt, J. C. (ed.), *Domesday Studies* (Woodbridge: The Boydell Press, 1987)

Le Patourel, J., *The Norman Empire* (Oxford: OUP, 1976)

Stafford, P., *Unification and Conquest* (London: Edward Arnold, 1989)

Stenton, F. M., *Anglo-Saxon England*, 3rd edn (Oxford: OUP, 1971)

Strickland, M. (ed.), *Anglo-Norman Warfare* (Woodbridge: The Boydell Press, 1992)

Williams, A., *The English and the Norman Conquest* (Woodbridge: The Boydell Press, 1995)

2 The Norman kings

Barlow, F., *The Norman Conquest and Beyond* (Woodbridge: The Hambledon Press, 1987)

Bradbury, J., *Stephen and Matilda: The Civil War of 1139–53* (Stroud: Allan Sutton, 1996)

Douglas, D. C., *William the Conqueror* (London: Methuen, 1964)

3 Castles

Kenyon, J. R., *Medieval Fortifications* (London: Leicester University Press, 1990)

Platt, C., *The Castle in Medieval England and Wales* (London: Secker & Warburg, 1982)

Renn, D., *Norman Castles in Britain* (London: John Baker, 1968)

Thompson, M. W., *The Rise of the Castle* (Cambridge: CUP, 1991)

4 Towns

Ottaway, P., *Archaeology in British Towns* (London: Routledge, 1992)

Schofield, J. and Vince, A., *Medieval Towns* (London: Leicester University Press, 1994)

5 Churches and monasteries

Aston, M., *Monasteries* (London: Batsford, 1993)

Greene, J. P., *Medieval Monasteries* (London: Leicester University Press, 1992)

Knowles, D., *The Religious Orders in England*, 3rd edn, 3 vols (Cambridge: CUP, 1959)

Macready, S. and Thompson, F. H., *Art and Patronage in the English Romanesque* (London: The Society of Antiquaries of London, 1986)

Morris, R., *Cathedrals and Abbeys of England & Wales* (London: Dent, 1979)

Zarnecki, G., *Romanesque* (London: Universe Books, 1971)

6 The Norman countryside

Aston, M., *Interpreting the Landscape* (London: Batsford, 1985)

Bond, J. and Tiller, K. (eds), *Blenheim: Landscape for a Palace* (Gloucester: Allan Sutton and Oxford University Department for External Studies, 1987)

Index

(Page numbers in **bold** refer to illustrations)

The Author

Trevor Rowley is Deputy Director of the Department for Continuing Education at Oxford University. He has combined his career in Adult Education with a lifelong love of landscape history and archaeology which began as a postgraduate student under the supervision of W. G. Hoskins at Oxford. His publications include *Villages in the Landscape*, *The High Middle Ages* and *The Norman Heritage*. He has excavated in Britain and elsewhere in Europe and is an enthusiastic traveller. He is fascinated by the Norman enigma about which he continues to research.

'One of the great classic series of British archaeology.' *Current Archaeology*

This volume is part of a major series, jointly conceived for English Heritage and Batsford, under the general editorship of Dr Stephen Johnson at English Heritage.

Titles in the series:

Sites
Avebury Caroline Malone
Danebury Barry Cunliffe
Dover Castle Jonathan Coad
Flag Fen: Prehistoric Fenland Centre Francis Pryor
Fountains Abbey Glyn Coppack
Glastonbury Philip Rahtz
Hadrian's Wall Stephen Johnson
Housesteads James Crow
Ironbridge Gorge Catherine Clark
Lindisfarne Deirdre O'Sullivan and Robert Young
Maiden Castle Niall M. Sharples
Roman Bath Barry Cunliffe
Roman London Gustav Milne
Roman York Patrick Ottaway
St Augustine's Abbey, Canterbury Richard Gem et al.
Stonehenge Julian Richards
Tintagel Charles Thomas
The Tower of London Geoffrey Parnell
Viking Age York Richard Hall
Wharram Percy: Deserted Medieval Village Maurice Beresford and John Hurst

Periods
Anglo-Saxon England Martin Welch
Bronze Age Britain Michael Parker Pearson
Industrial England Michael Stratton and Barrie Trinder
Iron Age Britain Barry Cunliffe
Norman England Trevor Rowley
Roman Britain Martin Millett
Stone Age Britain Nicholas Barton
Viking Age England Julian D. Richards

Subjects
Abbeys and Priories Glyn Coppack
Canals Nigel Crowe
Castles Tom McNeill
Channel Defences Andrew Saunders
Church Archaeology Warwick Rodwell
Life in Roman Britain Joan Alcock
Prehistoric Settlements Robert Bewley
Roman Forts in Britain Paul Bidwell
Roman Towns in Britain Guy de la Bédoyère
Roman Villas and the Countryside Guy de la Bédoyère
Ships and Shipwrecks Peter Marsden
Shrines and Sacrifice Ann Woodward
Victorian Churches James Stevens Curl

Towns
Canterbury Marjorie Lyle
Chester Peter Carrington
Durham Martin Roberts
Norwich Brian Ayers
Winchester Tom Beaumont James
York Richard Hall

Landscapes through Time
Dartmoor Sandy Gerrard
Peak District John Barnatt and Ken Smith
Yorkshire Dales Robert White
Forthcoming
Lake District Robert Bewley